The Lesser Key of Solomon

GOETIA

CONTAINS TWO HUNDRED DIAGRAMS AND SEALS
FOR INVOCATION AND CONVOCATION OF SPIRITS.
NECROMANCY, WITCHCRAFT AND BLACK ART.
TRANSLATED FROM ANCIENT MANUSCRIPTS IN THE
BRITISH MUSEUM, LONDON

by

Samuel Liddell MacGregor Mathers

and

Aleister Crowley

ΕΠΙΚΑΛΟΥΜΑΙ ΣΕ ΤΟΝ ΕΝ ΤΩ ΚΕΝΕΩ ΠΝΕΥΜΑΤΙ, ΔΕΙΝΟΝ, ΑΟΡΑΤΟΝ, ΠΑΝΟΤΡΑΤΟΡΑ, ΘΕΟΝ ΘΕΩΝ, ΦΘΕΡΟΠΟΙΟΝ, ΚΑΙ ΕΠΗΜΟΠΟΙΝ, Ο ΜΙΣΩΝ ΟΙΚΙΑΝ ΕΥΣΤΑΘΟΥΣΑΝ, ΩΣ ΕΞΕΒΡΑΣΘΗΣ ΕΚ ΤΗΣ ΑΙΓΥΠΤΙΟΥ ΚΑΙ ΕΞΩ ΧΩΡΑΣ.

ΕΠΟΝΟΜΑΣΘΗΣ Ο ΠΑΝΤΑ ΠΗΣΣΩΝ ΚΑΙ ΜΗ ΝΙΚΩΜΕΝΟΣ.

ΕΠΙΚΑΛΟΥΜΑΙ ΣΕ ΤΥΦΩΝ ΣΗΘ ΤΑΣ ΣΑΣ ΜΑΤΡΕΙΑΣ ΕΠΙΤΕΛΩ, ΟΤΙ ΕΠΙΚΑΛΟΥΜΑΙ ΣΕ ΤΟ ΣΟΝ ΑΥΘΕΝΤΙΚΟΝ ΣΟΥ ΟΝΟΜΑ ΕΝ ΟΙΣ ΟΥ ΔΥΝΗ ΠΑΡΑΚΟΥΣΑΙ ΙΩΕΡΒΗΘ, ΙΩΠΑΚΕΡΒΗΟ, ΙΩΒΟΛΧΩΣΗΘ, ΙΩΠΑΤΑΘΝΑΖ, ΙΩΣΩΡΩ, ΙΩΝΕΒΟΥΤΟΣΟΥΑΛΗΘ, ΑΚΤΙΩΦΙ, ΕΡΕΣΧΙΓΑΛ, ΝΕΒΟΠΟΩΑΛΗΘ, ΑΒΕΡΑΜΕΝΘΩΟΝ, ΛΕΡΘΕΞΑΝΑΞ, ΕΘΡΕΛΥΩΘ, ΝΕΜΑΡΕΒΑ, ΑΕΜΙΝΑ, ΟΛΟΝ ΗΚΕ ΜΟΙ ΚΑΙ ΒΑΔΙΣΟΝ ΚΑΙ ΚΑΤΕΒΑΛΕ ΤΟΝ ΔΕΙΝΟΝ ΜΑΘΕΡΣ. ΡΙΓΕΙ ΚΑΙ ΠΥΡΕΙΩ ΑΥΤΟΣ ΗΔΙΚΗΣΕΝ ΤΟΝ ΑΝΘΡΩΠΟΝ ΚΑΙ ΤΟ ΑΙΜΑ ΤΟΥ ΦΥΩΝΟΣ ΕΣΚΕΧΥΣΕΝ ΠΑΡ'ΕΑΥΤΩ.

ΔΙΑ ΤΟΥΤΟ ΤΑΥΤΑ ΠΟΙΕΩ ΚΟΙΝΑ.

PREFACE

This translation of the FIRST BOOK of the "Lemegeton" which is now for the first time made accessible to students of TALISMANIC MAGIC was done, after careful collation and edition, from numerous Ancient Manuscripts in Hebrew, Latin, and French, by G. H. Fra. D.D.C.F., by the order of the Secret Chief of the Rosicrucian Order. The G. H. Fra., having succumbed unhappily to the assaults of the Four Great Princes (acting notably under Martial influences), it seemed expedient that the work should be brought to its conclusion by another hand. The investigation of a competent Skryer into the house of our unhappy Fra., confirmed this divination; neither our Fra. nor his Hermetic Mul. were there seen; but only the terrible shapes of the evil Adepts S.V.A. and H., whose original bodies having been sequestered by Justice, were no longer of use to them. On this we stayed no longer Our Hand; but withdrawing Ourselves, and consulting the Rota, and the Books M. and Q. did decide to ask Mr. Aleister Crowley, a poet, and skilled student of Magical Lore, and an expert Kabbalist, to complete openly that which had been begun in secret. This is that which is written: "His Bishoprick let another take." And again: "Oculi Tetragammaton." This is also that which is said: "Nomen Secundum refertur ad Gebhurah; qui est Rex Bittul atque Corruptio Achurajim Patris et Matris hoc indigitatur."

And so saying we wish you well.

Ex Deo Nascimur.
In Jesu Morimur.
Per S.S. Reviviscimus.

Given forth from our Mountain of A.,
this day of C.C. 1903 A. D.

PRELIMINARY INVOCATION

Thee I invoke, the Bornless one.
Thee that didst create the Earth and the Heavens:
Thee that didst create the Night and the Day.
Thee that didst create the Darkness and the Light.
Thou art Osorronophris: Whom no man has seen at any time.
Thou art Jäbas
Thou art Jäpôs:
Thou hast distinguished between the Just and the Unjust.
Thou didst make the Female and the Male.
Thou didst produce the Seed and the Fruit.
Thou didst form Men to love one another, and to hate one
another.

I am Mosheh Thy Prophet, unto Whom Thou didst commit Thy
Mysteries, the Ceremonies of Ishrael:
Thou didst produce the moist and the, dry, and that which
nourisheth all created Life.
Hear Thou Me, for I am the Angel of Paphrô Osorronophris: this
is Thy True Name, handed down to the Prophets of Ishrael.

Hear Me:--
Ar: Thiao: Rheibet: Atheleberseth:
A: Blatha: Abeu: Ebeu: Phi:
Thitasoe: Ib: Thiao.
Hear Me, and make all Spirits subject unto Me: so that every Spirit
of the Firmament and of the Ether; upon the Earth and under the
Earth: on dry Land and in the Water: of Whirling Air, and of
rushing Fire: and every Spell and Scourge of God may be obedient
unto Me.

7

I invoke Thee, the Terrible and Invisible God: Who dwellest in the
Void Place of the Spirit:--
Arogogorobraô: Sothou:
Modoriô: Phalarthaô: Döö: Apé, The Bornless One:
Hear Me: etc.

Hear me:--
Roubriaô: Mariôdam: Balbnabaoth: Assalonai: Aphniaô: I: Thoteth:
Abrasar: Aëôôü: Ischure, Mighty and Bornless One!
Hear me: etc.

I invoke thee:--
Ma: Barraiô: Jôêl: Kotha:
Athorêbalô: Abraoth:
Hear Me: etc.

Hear me!
Aôth: Abaôth: Basum: Isak:
Sabaoth: Iao:

This is the Lord of the Gods:
This is the Lord of the Universe:
This is He Whom the Winds fear.
This is He, Who having made Voice by His Commandment, is
Lord of All Things; King, Ruler and Helper.
Hear Me, etc.

Hear Me:--
Ieou: Pûr: Iou: Pûr: Iaôt: Iaeô: Ioou: Abrasar: Sabriam: Do: Uu:
Adonaie: Ede: Edu: Angelos ton Theon: Aniaia Lai: Gaia: Ape:
Diathanna Thorun.

I am He! the Bornless Spirit! having sight in the feet: Strong, and
the Immortal Fire!
I am He! the Truth!
I am He! Who hate that evil should be wrought in the, World!
I am He, that lighteneth and thundereth.
I am He, from Whom is the Shower of the Life of Earth:
I am He, Whose mouth ever flameth:
I am He, the Begetter and Manifester unto the Light:

I am He; the Grace of the World:

"The Heart Girt with a Serpent" is My Name!

Come Thou forth, and follow Me: and make all Spirits subject
unto Me so that every Spirit of the Firmament, and of the Ether:
upon the Earth and under the Earth: on dry Land, or in the Water:
of whirling Air or of rushing Fire: and every Spell and Scourge of
God, may be obedient unto Me!

Iao: Sabao:

Such are the Words!

THE INITIATED INTERPRETATION OF CEREMONIAL MAGIC

It is loftily amusing to the student of Magical literature who is not quite a fool--and rare is such a combination!--to note the criticism directed by the Philistine against the citadel of his science. Truly, since our childhood has ingrained into us not only literal belief in the Bible, but also substantial belief in Alf Laylah wa Laylah, and only adolescence can cure us, we are only too liable, in the rush and energy of dawning manhood, to overturn roughly and rashly both these classics, to regard them both on the same level, as interesting documents from the standpoint of folk-lore and anthropology, and as nothing more.

Even when we learn that the Bible, by a profound and minute study of the text, may be forced to yield up Qabalistic arcana of cosmic scope and importance, we are too often slow to apply a similar restorative to the companion volume, even if we are the luck holders of Burton's veritable edition.

To me, then, it remains to raise the Alf Laylah wa Laylah into its proper place once more.

I am not concerned to deny the objective reality of all "magical" phenomena; if they are illusions, they are at least as real as many unquestioned facts of daily life; and, if we follow Herbert Spencer, they are at least evidence of some cause.

Now, this fact is our base. What is the cause of my illusion of seeing a spirit in the triangle of Art?

Every smatterer, every expert in psychology, will answer: "That cause lies in your brain."

English children (pace the Education Act) are taught that the Universe lies in infinite Space; Hindu children, in the Akasa, which is the same thing.

Those Europeans who go a little deeper learn from Fichte, that the phenomenal Universe is the creation of the Ego; Hindus, or Europeans studying under Hindu Gurus, are told, that by Akasa is meant the Chitakasa. The Chitakasa is situated in the "Third Eye," i.e., in the brain. By assuming higher dimensions of space, we can assimilate this fact to Realism; but we have no need to take so much trouble.

This being true for the ordinary Universe, that all sense-impressions are dependent on changes in the brain, we must include illusions, which are after all sense-impressions as much as "realities" are, in the class of "phenomena dependent on brain-changes."

Magical phenomena, however, come under a special sub-class, since they are willed, and their cause is the series of "real" phenomena, called the operations of ceremonial Magic.

These consist of

(1) Sight.
The circle, square, triangle, vessels, lamps, robes, implements, etc.

(2) Sound.
The invocations.

(3) Smell.
The perfumes.

(4) Taste.
The Sacraments.

(5) Touch.
As under (1).

(6) Mind.

The combination of all these and reflection on their significance.

These unusual impressions (1-5) produce unusual brain-changes; hence their summary (6) is of unusual kind. Its projection back into the apparently phenomenal world is therefore unusual.

Herein then consists the reality of the operations and effects of ceremonial magic, and I conceive that the apology is ample, as far as the "effects" refer only to those phenomena which appear to the magician himself, the appearance of the spirit, his conversation, possible shocks from imprudence, and so on, even to ecstasy on the one hand, and death or madness on the other.

But can any of the effects described in this our book Goetia be obtained, and if so, can you give a rational explanation of the circumstances? Say you so?

I can, and will.

The spirits of the Goetia are portions of the human brain.

Their seals therefore represent (Mr. Spencer's projected cube) methods of stimulating or regulating those particular spots (through the eye).

The names of God are vibrations calculated to establish:

(a) General control of the brain., (Establishment of functions relative to the subtle world.)

(b) Control over the brain in detail. (Rank or type of the Spirit.)

(c) Control of one special portion. (Name of the Spirit.)

The perfumes aid this through smell. Usually the perfume will only tend to control a large area; but there is an attribution of perfumes to letters of the alphabet enabling one, by a Qabalistic formula, to spell out the Spirit's name.

I need not enter into more particular discussion of these points; the intelligent reader can easily fill in what is lacking.

If, then, I say, with Solomon:

"The Spirit Cimieries teaches logic," what I mean is:

"Those portions of my brain which subserve the logical faculty may be stimulated and developed by following out the processes called 'The Invocation of Cimieries.'"

And this is a purely materialistic rational statement; it is independent of any objective hierarchy at all. Philosophy has nothing to say; and Science can only suspend judgment, pending a proper and methodical investigation of the facts alleged.

Unfortunately, we cannot stop there. Solomon promises us that we can (1) obtain information; (2) destroy our enemies; (3) understand the voices of nature; (4) obtain treasure; (5) heal diseases, etc. I have taken

these five powers at random; considerations of space forbid me to explain all.

(1) Brings up facts from sub-consciousness.

(2) Here we come to an interesting fact. It is curious to note the contrast between the noble means and the apparently vile ends of magical rituals. The latter are disguises for sublime truths. "To destroy our enemies" is to realize the illusion of duality, to excite compassion.

(Ah! Mr. Waite, the world of Magic is a mirror, wherein who sees muck is muck.)

(3) A careful naturalist will understand much from the voices of the animals he has studied long. Even a child knows the difference of a cat's miauling and purring. The faculty may be greatly developed.

(4) Business capacity may be stimulated.

(5) Abnormal states of the body may be corrected, and the involved tissues brought back to tone, in obedience to currents started from the brain.

So for all other phenomena. There is no effect which is truly and necessarily miraculous.

Our Ceremonial Magic fines down, then, to a series of minute, though of course empirical, physiological experiments, and whoso, will carry them through intelligently need not fear the result.

I have all the health, and treasure, and logic, I need; I have no time to waste. "There is a lion in the way." For me these practices are useless; but for the benefit of others less fortunate I give them to the world, together with this explanation of, and apology for, them.

I trust that the explanation will enable many students who have hitherto, by a puerile objectivity in their view of the question, obtained no results, to succeed; that the apology may impress upon our scornful men of science that the study of the bacillus should give place to that

of the baculum, the little to the great--how great one only realizes when one identifies the wand with the Mahalingam, up which Brahma flew at the rate of 84,000 yojanas a second for 84,000 mahakalpas, down which Vishnu flew at the rate of 84,000 croces of yojanas a second for 84,000 crores of mahakalpas--yet neither reached an end.

But I reach an end.

Boleskine House,
   Foyers, N.B.

PRELIMINARY DEFINITION OF MAGIC

LEMEGETON VEL CLAVICULA SALOMONIS REGIS

MAGIC is the Highest, most Absolute, and most Divine Knowledge of Natural Philosophy, 1 advanced in its works and wonderful operations by a right understanding of the inward and occult virtue of things; so that true Agents 2 being applied to proper Patients, 3 strange and admirable effects will thereby be produced. Whence magicians are profound and diligent searchers into Nature; they, because of their skill, know how to anticipate an effort, 4 the which to the vulgar shall seem to be a miracle.

Origen saith that the Magical Art doth not contain anything subsisting, but although it should, yet that it must not be Evil, or subject to contempt or scorn; and doth distinguish the Natural Magic from that which is Diabolical.

Apollonius Tyannaeus only exercised the Natural Magic, by the which he did perform wonderful things.

Philo Hebraeus saith that true Magic, by which we do arrive at the understanding of the Secret Works of Nature, is so far from being contemptible that the greatest Monarchs and Kings have studied it. Nay! among the Persians none might reign unless he was skilful in this GREAT ART.

This Noble Science often degenerateth, from Natural becometh Diabolical, and from True Philosophy turneth unto Nigromancy. 1 The which is wholly to be charged upon its followers, who, abusing or not being capable of that High and Mystical Knowledge do immediately hearken unto the temptations of Sathan, and are misled by him into the Study of the Black Art. Hence it is that Magic lieth under disgrace, and they who seek after it are vulgarly esteemed Sorcerers.

The Fraternity of the Rosie Crusians thought it not fit to style themselves Magicians, but rather Philosophers. And they be not ignorant Empiricks, 2 but learned and experienced Physicians, whose remedies be not only Lawful but Divine.

THE BRIEF INTRODUCTORY DESCRIPTION

(N.B. This is taken from several MS. Codices, of which the four principal variations are here composed together in parallel columns as an example of the close agreement of the various texts of the Lemegeton.

For in the whole work the differences in the wording of the various Codices are not sufficient to require the constant giving of parallel readings; but except in the more ancient examples there is much deterioration in the Seals and Sigils, so that in this latter respect the more recent exemplars are not entirely reliable.)

CLAVICULA SALOMONIS REGIS,
which containeth all the Names, Offices, and Orders of all the Spirits that ever he had converse with, with the Seals and Characters to each Spirit and the manner of calling them forth to visible appearance:

In 5 parts, viz.:

(1) **THE FIRST PART** is a Book of Evil Spirits, called **GOETIA**, showing how he bound up those Spirits, and used them in general things, whereby he obtained great fame.

(2) **THE SECOND PART** is a Book of Spirits, partly Evil and partly Good, which is named **THEURGIA-GOETIA**, all Aërial Spirits, etc.

(3) **THE THIRD PART** is of Spirits governing the Planetary Hours, and what Spirits belong to every degree, of the Signs, and Planets in the Signs. Called the **PAULINE ART**, etc.

(4) **THE FOURTH PART** of this Book is called **ALMADEL** or **SOLOMON**, which containeth those Spirits which govern the Four Altitudes, or the 360 Degrees of the Zodiac.

These two last Orders of Spirits are Good, and to be sought for by Divine seeking, etc., and are called **THEURGIA**.

(5) **THE FIFTH PART** is a Book of Orations and Prayers that Wise Solomon used upon the Altar in the Temple. The which is called **ARS NOVA**, which was revealed unto Solomon by that Holy Angel of God called MICHAEL; and he also received many brief Notes written with the Finger of God, which were declared to him by the said Angel with Claps of Thunder; without which Notes King Solomon had never obtained his great knowledge, for by them in a short time he knew all Arts and Sciences both Good and Bad; from these Notes it is called the **NOTARY ART**, etc.

THE WHOLE LEMEGETON OR CLAVICULA

Now this Book containeth all the Names, Orders, and Offices of all the Spirits with which Solomon ever conversed, the Seals and Characters belonging to each Spirit, and the manner of calling them forth to visible appearance:

Divided into 5 special Books or parts, viz.:

(1) **THE FIRST BOOK**, or **PART**, which is a Book concerning Spirits of Evil, and which is termed **THE GOETIA OF SOLOMON**, sheweth forth his manner of binding these Spirits for use in things divers. And hereby did he acquire great renown.

(2) **THE SECOND BOOK** is one which treateth of Spirits mingled of Good and Evil Natures, the which is entitled **THE THEURGIA-GOETIA**, or the Magical Wisdom of the Spirits Aërial, whereof some do abide, but certain do wander and abide not.

(3) **THE THIRD BOOK**, called **ARS PAULINA**, or **THE ART PAULINE**, treateth of the Spirits allotted unto every degree of the 360 Degrees of the Zodiac; and also of the Signs, and of the Planets in the Signs, as well as of the Hours.

(4) **THE FOURTH BOOK**, called **ARS ALMADEL SALOMONIS**, or **THE ART ALMADEL OF SOLOMON**, concerneth those Spirits which be set over the Quaternary of the Altitudes.

These two last mentioned Books, the **ART PAULINE** and the **ART ALMADEL**, do relate unto Good Spirits alone, whose knowledge is to be obtained through seeking unto the Divine. These two Books be also classed together under the Name of the First and Second Parts of the Book **THEURGIA OF SOLOMON**.

(5) **THE FIFTH BOOK** of the Lemegeton is one of Prayers and Orations. The which Solomon the Wise did use upon the Altar in

the Temple. And the titles hereof be **ARS NOVA**, the **NEW ART**, and **ARS NOTARIA**, the **NOTARY ART**. The which was revealed to him by **MICHAEL**, that Holy Angel of God, in thunder and in lightning, and he further did receive by the aforesaid Angel certain Notes written by the Hand of God, without the which that Great King had never attained unto his great Wisdom, for thus he knew all things and all Sciences and Arts whether Good or Evil.

THE BOOK OF EVIL SPIRITS

THE KEY OF SOLOMON, which contains all the names, orders, and offices of all the Spirits that ever Solomon conversed with, together with the Seals and Characters belonging to each Spirit, and the manner of calling them forth to visible appearance:

In 4 parts.

(1) **THE FIRST PART** is a Book of Evil Spirits, called **GOETIA**, showing how he bound up those Spirits and used them in several things, whereby he obtained great fame.

(2) **THE SECOND PART** is a Book of Spirits, partly Good and partly Evil, which is named **THEURGIA-GOETIA**, all Aërial Spirits, etc.

(3) **THE: THIRD PART** is a Book governing the Planetary Houses, and what Spirits belong to every Degree of the Signs, and Planets in the Signs. Called the Pauline Art.

(4) **THE FOURTH PART** is a Book called the **ALMADEL OF SOLOMON**, which contains Twenty Chief Spirits who govern the Four Altitudes, or the 360 Degrees of the Zodiac.

These two last Orders of Spirits are Good, and called **THEURGIA**, and are to be sought after by Divine seeking.

These Most Sacred Mysteries were revealed unto Solomon.

Now in this Book **LEMEGETON** is contained the whole Art of King Solomon. And although there be many other Books that are said to be his, yet none is to be compared hereunto, for this containeth them all. Though there be titles with several other Names of the Book, as **THE BOOK HELISOL**, which is the very same with this last Book of Lemegeton called **ARS NOVA** or **ARS NOTARIA**, etc.

These Books were first found in the Chaldee and Hebrew Tongues at Jerusalem by a Jewish Rabbi; and by him put into the Greek language and thence into the Latin, as it is said.

SHEMHAMPHORASH

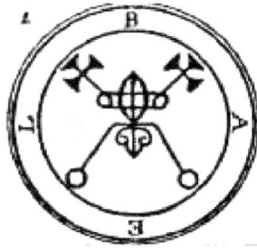

(1.) BAEL.

The First Principal Spirit is a King ruling in the East, called Bael. He maketh thee to go Invisible. He ruleth over 66 Legions of Infernal Spirits. He appeareth in divers shapes, sometimes like a Cat, sometimes like a Toad, and sometimes like a Man, and sometimes all these forms at once. He speaketh hoarsely. This is his character which is used to be worn as a Lamen before him who calleth him forth, or else he will not do thee homage.

(2.) AGARES.

The Second Spirit is a Duke called Agreas, or Agares. He is under the Power of the East, and cometh up in the form of an old fair Man, riding upon a Crocodile, carrying a Goshawk upon his fist, and yet mild in appearance. He maketh them to run that stand still, and bringeth back runaways. He teaches all Languages or Tongues presently. He hath power also to destroy Dignities both Spiritual and Temporal, and causeth Earthquakes. He was of the Order of Virtues. He hath under his government 31 Legions of Spirits. And this is his Seal or Character which thou shalt wear as a Lamen before thee.

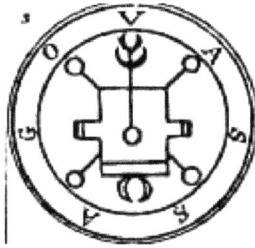

(3.)VASSAGO.

The Third Spirit is a Mighty Prince, being of the same nature as Agares. He is called Vassago. This Spirit is of a Good Nature, and his office is to declare things Past and to Come, and to discover all things Hid or Lost. And he governeth 26 Legions of Spirits, and this is his Seal.

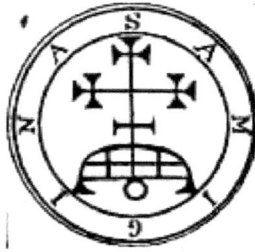

(4.) SAMIGINA, OR GAMIGM.

The Fourth Spirit is Samigina, a Great Marquis. He appeareth in the form of a little Horse or Ass, and then into Human shape doth he change himself at the request of the Master. He speaketh with a hoarse voice. He ruleth over 30 Legions of Inferiors. He teaches all Liberal Sciences, and giveth account of Dead Souls that died in sin. And his Seal is this, which is to be worn before the Magician when he is Invocator, etc.

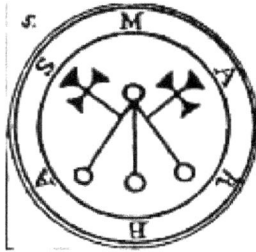

(5.) MARBAS.

The fifth Spirit is Marbas. He is a Great President, and appeareth at first in the form of a Great Lion, but afterwards, at the request of the Master, he putteth on Human Shape. He answereth truly of things Hidden or Secret. He causeth Diseases and cureth them. Again, he giveth great Wisdom and Knowledge in Mechanical Arts; and can change men into other shapes. He governeth 36 Legions of Spirits. And his Seal is this, which is to be worn as aforesaid.

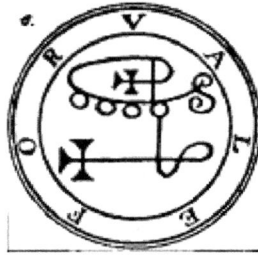

(6.) VALEFOR.

The Sixth Spirit is Valefor. He is a mighty Duke, and appeareth in the shape of a Lion with an Ass's Head, bellowing. He is a good Familiar, but tempteth them he is a familiar of to steal. He governeth 10 Legions of Spirits. His Seal is this, which is to be worn, whether thou wilt have him for a Familiar, or not.

(7.) AMON.

The Seventh Spirit is Amon. He is a Marquis great in power, and
most stern. He appeareth like a Wolf with a Serpents tail,
vomiting out of his mouth flames of fire; but at the command of
the Magician he putteth on the shape of a Man with Dog's teeth
beset in a head like a Raven; or else like a Man with a Raven's
head (simply). He telleth all things Past and to Come. He
procureth feuds and reconcileth controversies between friends.
He governeth 40 Legions of Spirits. His Seal is this which is to be
worn as aforesaid, etc.

(8.) BARBATOS.

The Eighth Spirit is Barbatos. He is a Great Duke, and appeareth when the Sun is in Sagittary, with four noble Kings and their companies of great troops. He giveth understanding of the singing of Birds, and of the Voices of other creatures, such as the barking of Dogs. He breaketh the Hidden Treasures open that have been laid by the Enchantments of Magicians. He is of the Order of Virtues, of which some part he retaineth still; and he knoweth all things Past, and to come, and conciliateth Friends and those that be in Power. He ruleth over 30 Legions of Spirits. His Seal of Obedience is this, the which wear before thee as aforesaid.

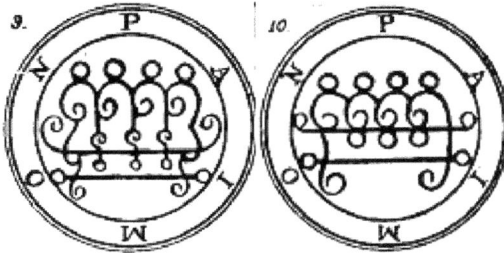

(9.) PAIMON.

The Ninth Spirit in this Order is Paimon, a Great King, and very obedient unto LUCIFER. He appeareth in the form of a Man sitting upon a Dromedary with a Crown most glorious upon his head. There goeth before him also an Host of Spirits, like Men with Trumpets and well sounding Cymbals, and all other sorts of Musical Instruments. He hath a great Voice, and roareth at his first coming, and his speech is such that the Magician cannot well understand unless he can compel him. This Spirit can teach all Arts and Sciences, and other secret things. He can discover unto thee what the Earth is, and what holdeth it up in the Waters; and what Mind is, and where it is; or any other thing thou mayest desire to know. He giveth Dignity, and confirmeth the same. He bindeth or maketh any man subject unto the Magician if he so desire it. He giveth good Familiars, and such as can teach all Arts. He is to be observed towards the West. He is of the Order of Dominations. 1 He hath under him 200 Legions of Spirits, and part of them are of the Order of Angels, and the other part of Potentates. Now if thou callest this Spirit Paimon alone, thou must make him some offering; and there will attend him two Kings called LABAL and ABALIM, and also other Spirits who be of the Order of Potentates in his Host, and 25 Legions. And those Spirits which be subject unto them are not always with them unless the Magician do compel them. His Character is this which must be worn as a Lamen before thee, etc.

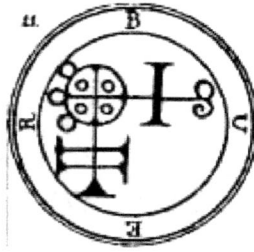

(10.) BUER.

The Tenth Spirit is Buer, a Great President. He appeareth in Sagittary, and that is his shape when the Sun is there. He teaches Philosophy, both Moral and Natural, and the Logic Art, and also the Virtues of all Herbs and Plants. He healeth all distempers in man, and giveth good Familiars. He governeth 50 Legions of Spirits, and his Character of obedience is this, which thou must wear when thou callest him forth unto appearance.

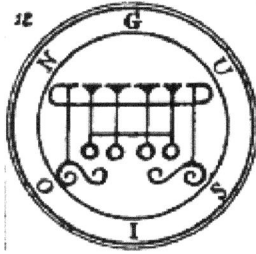

(11.) GUSION.

The Eleventh Spirit in order is a great and strong Duke, called Gusion. He appeareth like a Xenopilus. He telleth all things, Past, Present, and to Come, and showeth the meaning and resolution of all questions thou mayest ask. He conciliateth and reconcileth friendships, and giveth Honour and Dignity unto any. He ruleth over 40 Legions of Spirits. His Seal is this, the which wear thou as aforesaid.

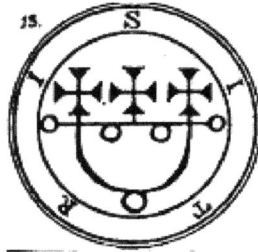

(12.) SITRI.

The Twelfth Spirit is Sitri. He is a Great Prince and appeareth at first with a Leopard's head and the Wings of a Gryphon, but after the command of the Master of the Exorcism he putteth on Human shape, and that very beautiful. He enflameth men with Women's love, and Women with Men's love; and causeth them also to show themselves naked if it be desired. He governeth 60 Legions of Spirits. His Seal is this, to be worn as a Lamen before thee, etc.

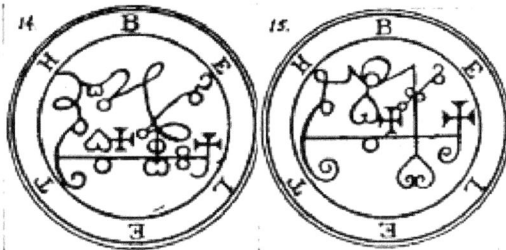

(13.)   BELETH.

The Thirteenth Spirit is called Beleth (or Bileth, or Bilet). He is a mighty King and terrible. He rideth on a pale horse with trumpets and other kinds of musical instruments playing before him. He is very furious at his first appearance, that is, while the Exorcist layeth his courage; for to do this he must hold a Hazel Wand in his hand, striking it out towards the South and East Quarters, make a triangle, Δ, without the Circle, and then command him into it by the Bonds and Charges of Spirits as hereafter followeth. And if he doth not enter into the triangle, Δ, at your threats, rehearse the Bonds and Charms before him, and then he will yield Obedience and come into it, and do what he is commanded by the Exorcist. Yet he must receive him courteously because he is a Great King, and do homage unto him, as the Kings and Princes do that attend upon him. And thou must have always a Silver Ring on the middle finger of the left hand held against thy face, 1 as they do yet before AMAYMON. This Great King Beleth causeth all the love that may be, both of Men and of Women, until the Master Exorcist hath had his desire fulfilled. He is of the Order of Powers, and he governeth 85 Legions of Spirits. His Noble Seal is this, which is to be worn before thee at working.

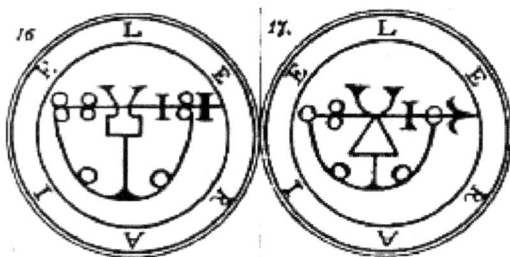

(14.) LERAJE, OR LERAIKHA.

The Fourteenth Spirit is called Leraje (or Leraie). He is a Marquis Great in Power, showing himself in the likeness of an Archer clad in Green, and carrying a Bow and Quiver. He causeth all great Battles and Contests; and maketh wounds to putrefy that are made with Arrows by Archers. This belongeth unto Sagittary. He governeth 30 Legions of Spirits, and this is his Seal, etc.

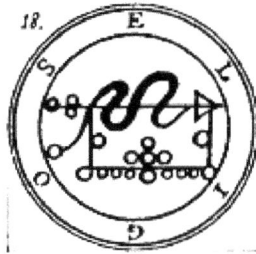

(15.) ELIGOS.

The Fifteenth Spirit in Order is Eligos, a Great Duke, and appeareth in the form of a goodly Knight, carrying a Lance, an Ensign, and a Serpent. He discovereth hidden things, and knoweth things to come; and of Wars, and how the Soldiers will or shall meet. He causeth the Love of Lords and Great Persons. He governeth 60 Legions of Spirits. His Seal is this, etc.

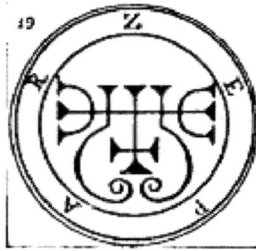

(16.) ZEPAR.

The Sixteenth Spirit is Zepar. He is a Great Duke, and appeareth in Red Apparel and Armour, like a Soldier. His office is to cause Women to love Men, and to bring them together in love. He also maketh them barren. He governeth 26 Legions of Inferior Spirits, and his Seal is this, which he obeyeth when he seeth it.

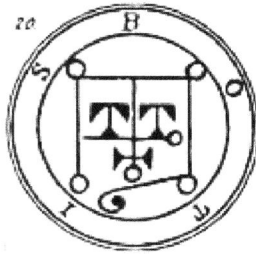

(17.) BOTIS.

The Seventeenth Spirit is Botis, a Great President, and an Earl. He appeareth at the first show in the form of an ugly Viper, then at the command of the Magician he putteth on a Human shape with Great Teeth, and two Horns, carrying a bright and sharp Sword in his hand. He telleth all things Past, and to Come, and reconcileth Friends and Foes. He ruleth over 60 Legions of Spirits, and this is his Seal, etc.

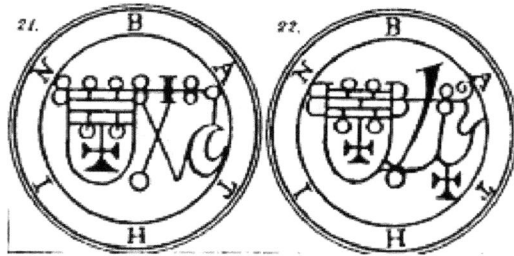

(18.) BATHIN.

The Eighteenth Spirit is Bathin. He is a Mighty and Strong Duke, and appeareth like a Strong Man with the tail of a Serpent, sitting upon a Pale-Coloured Horse. He knoweth the Virtues of Herbs and Precious Stones, and can transport men suddenly from one country to another. He ruleth over 30 Legions of Spirits. His Seal is this which is to be worn as aforesaid.

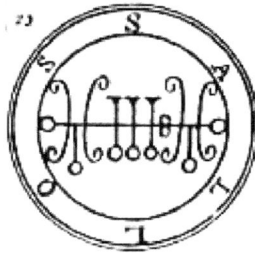

(19.) SALLOS.

The Nineteenth Spirit is Sallos (or Saleos). He is a Great and Mighty Duke, and appeareth in the form of a gallant Soldier riding on a Crocodile, with a Ducal Crown on his head, but peaceably. He causeth the Love of Women to Men, and of Men to Women; and governeth 30 Legions of Spirits. His Seal is this, etc.

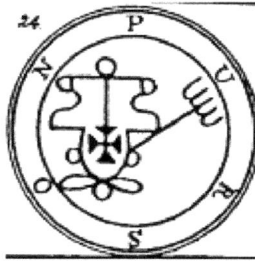

(20.) PURSON.

The Twentieth Spirit is Purson, a Great King. His appearance is comely, like a Man with a Lion's face, carrying a cruel Viper in his hand, and riding upon a Bear. Going before him are many Trumpets sounding. He knoweth all things hidden, and can discover Treasure, and tell all things Past, Present, and to Come. He can take a Body either Human or Aërial, and answereth truly of all Earthly things both Secret and Divine, and of the Creation of the World. He bringeth forth good Familiars, and under his Government there be 22 Legions of Spirits, partly of the Order of Virtues and partly of the Order of Thrones. His Mark, Seal, or Character is this, unto the which he oweth obedience, and which thou shalt wear in time of action, etc.

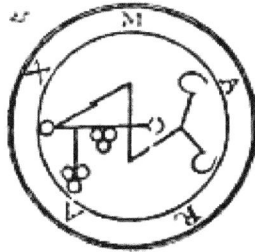

(21.) MARAX.

The Twenty-first Spirit is Marax. He is a Great Earl and President. He appeareth like a great Bull with a Man's face. His office is to make Men very knowing in Astronomy, and all other Liberal Sciences; also he can give good Familiars, and wise, knowing the virtues of Herbs and Stones which be precious. He governeth 30 Legions of Spirits, and his Seal is this, which must be made and worn as aforesaid, etc.

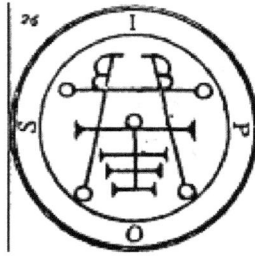

(22.) IPOS.

The Twenty-second Spirit is Ipos. He is an Earl, and a Mighty Prince, and appeareth in the form of an Angel with a Lion's Head, and a Goose's Foot, and Hare's Tail. He knoweth all things Past, Present, and to Come. He maketh men witty and bold.

He governeth 36 Legions of Spirits. His Seal is this, which thou shalt wear, etc.

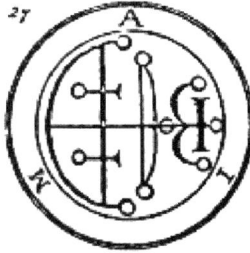

(23.) AIM.

The Twenty-third Spirit is Aim. He is a Great Strong Duke. He appeareth in the form of a very handsome Man in body, but with three Heads; the first, like a Serpent, the second like a Man having two Stars on his Forehead, the third like a Calf. He rideth on a Viper, carrying a Firebrand in his Hand, wherewith he setteth cities, castles, and great Places, on fire. He maketh thee witty in all manner of ways, and giveth true answers unto private matters. He governeth 26 Legions of Inferior Spirits; and his Seal is this, which wear thou as aforesaid, etc.

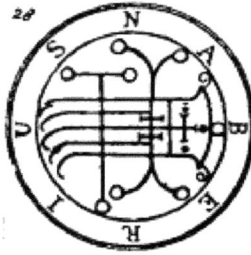

(24.) NABERIUS.

The Twenty-fourth Spirit is Naberius. He is a most valiant Marquis, and showeth in the form of a Black Crane, fluttering about the Circle, and when he speaketh it is with a hoarse voice. He maketh men cunning in all Arts and Sciences, but especially in the Art of Rhetoric. He restoreth lost Dignities and Honours. He governeth 19 Legions of Spirits. His Seal is this, which is to be worn, etc.

(25.) GLASYA-LABOLAS.

The Twenty-fifth Spirit is Glasya-Labolas. He is a Mighty President and Earl, and showeth himself in the form of a Dog with Wings like a Gryphon. He teacheth all Arts and Sciences in an instant, and is an Author of Bloodshed and Manslaughter. He teacheth all things Past, and to Come. If desired he causeth the love both of Friends and of Foes. He can make a Man to go Invisible. And he hath under his command 36 Legions of Spirits. His Seal is this, to be, etc.

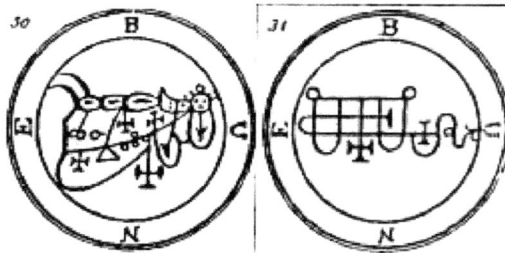

(26.) BUNE, OR BIMÉ.

The Twenty-sixth Spirit is Buné (or Bim). He is a Strong, Great and Mighty Duke. He appeareth in the form of a Dragon with three heads, one like a Dog, one like a Gryphon, and one like a Man. He speaketh with a high and comely Voice. He changeth the Place of the Dead, and causeth the Spirits which be under him to gather together upon your Sepulchres. He giveth Riches unto a Man, and maketh him Wise and Eloquent. He giveth true Answers unto Demands. And he governeth 30 Legions of Spirits. His Seal is this, unto the which he oweth Obedience. He hath another Seal (which is the first of these, but the last is the best)

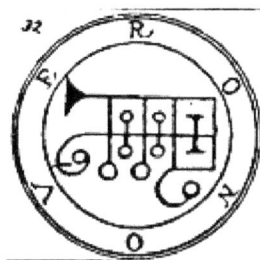

(27.) RONOVÉ.

The Twenty-seventh Spirit is Ronové. He appeareth in the Form of a Monster. He teacheth the Art of Rhetoric very well and giveth Good Servants, Knowledge of Tongues, and Favours with Friends or Foes. He is a Marquis and Great Earl; and there be under his command 19 Legions of Spirits. His Seal is this, etc.

(28.) BERITH.

The Twenty-eighth Spirit in Order, as Solomon bound them, is named Berith. He is a Mighty, Great, and Terrible Duke. He hath two other Names given unto him by men of later times, viz.: BEALE, or BEAL, and BOFRY or BOLFRY. He appeareth in the Form of a Soldier with Red Clothing, riding upon a Red Horse, and having a Crown of Gold upon his head. He giveth true answers, Past, Present, and to Come. Thou must make use of a Ring in calling him forth, as is before spoken of regarding Beleth. 3 He can turn all metals into Gold. He can give Dignities, and can confirm them unto Man. He speaketh with a very clear and subtle Voice. He governeth 26 Legions of Spirits. His Seal is this, etc.

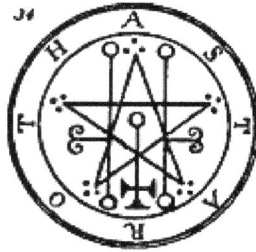

(29.) ASTAROTH.

The Twenty.--ninth Spirit is Astaroth. He is a Mighty, Strong Duke, and appeareth in the Form of an hurtful Angel riding on an Infernal Beast like a Dragon, and carrying in his right hand a Viper. Thou must in no wise let him approach too near unto thee, lest he do thee damage by his Noisome Breath. Wherefore the Magician must hold the Magical Ring near his face, and that will defend him. He giveth true answers of things Past, Present, and to Come, and can discover all Secrets. He will declare wittingly how the Spirits fell, if desired, and the reason of his own fall. He can make men wonderfully knowing in all Liberal Sciences. He ruleth 40 Legions of Spirits. His Seal is this, which wear thou as a Lamen before thee, or else he will not appear nor yet obey thee, etc.

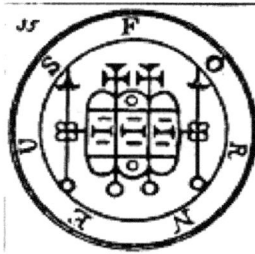

(30.) FORNEUS.

The Thirtieth Spirit is Forneus. He is a Mighty and Great Marquis, and appeareth in the Form of a Great Sea-Monster. He teacheth, and maketh men wonderfully knowing in the Art of Rhetoric. He causeth men to have a Good Name, and to have the knowledge and understanding of Tongues. He maketh one to be beloved of his Foes as well as of his Friends. He governeth 29 Legions of Spirits, partly of the Order of Thrones, and partly of that of Angels. His Seal is this, which wear thou, etc.

(31.) FORAS.

The Thirty-first Spirit is Foras. He is a Mighty President, and appeareth in the Form of a Strong Man in Human Shape. He can give the understanding to Men how they may know the Virtues of all Herbs and Precious Stones. He teacheth the Arts of Logic and Ethics in all their parts. If desired he maketh men invisible, 1 and to live long, and to be eloquent. He can discover Treasures and recover things Lost. He ruleth over 29 Legions of Spirits, and his Seal is this, which wear thou, etc.

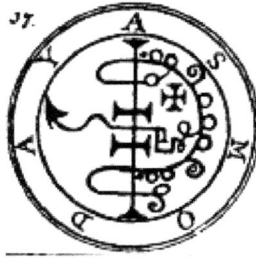

(32.) ASMODAY.

The Thirty-second Spirit is Asmoday, or Asmodai. He is a Great King, Strong, and Powerful. He appeareth with Three Heads, whereof the first is like a Bull, the second like a Man, and the third like a Ram; he bath also the tail of a Serpent, and from his mouth issue Flames of Fire. His Feet are webbed like those of a Goose. He sitteth upon an Infernal Dragon, and beareth in his hand a Lance with a Banner. He is first and choicest under the Power of AMAYMON, he goeth before all other. When the Exorcist bath a mind to call him, let it be abroad, and let him stand on his feet all the time of action, with his Cap or Headdress off; for if it be on, AMAYMON will deceive him and call all his actions to be bewrayed. But as soon as the Exorcist seeth Asmoday in the shape aforesaid, he shall call him by his Name, saying: "Art thou Asmoday?" and he will not deny it, and by-and-by he will bow down unto the ground. He giveth the Ring of Virtues; he teacheth the Arts of Arithmetic, Astronomy, Geometry, and all handicrafts absolutely. He giveth true and full answers unto thy demands. He maketh one Invincible. He showeth the place where Treasures lie, and guardeth it. He, amongst the Legions of AMAYMON governeth 72 Legions of Spirits Inferior. His Seal is this which thou must wear as a Lamen upon thy breast, etc.

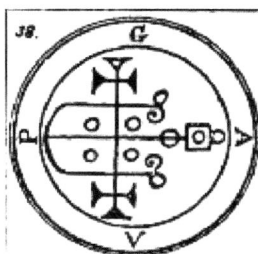

(33.) GAAP.

The Thirty-third Spirit is Gaap. He is a Great President and a Mighty Prince. He appeareth when the Sun is in some of the Southern Signs, in a Human Shape, going before Four Great and Mighty Kings, as if he were a Guide to conduct them along on their way. His Office is to make men Insensible or Ignorant; as also in Philosophy to make them Knowing, and in all the Liberal Sciences. He can cause Love or Hatred, also he can teach thee to consecrate those things that belong to the Dominion of AMAYMON his King. He can deliver Familiars out of the Custody of other Magicians, and answereth truly and perfectly of things Past, Present, and to Come. He can carry and re-carry men very speedily from one Kingdom to another, at the Will and Pleasure of the Exorcist. He ruleth over 66 Legions of Spirits, and he was of the Order of Potentates. His Seal is this to be made and to be worn as aforesaid, etc.

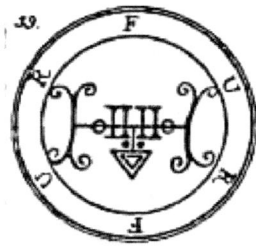

(34.) FURFUR.

The Thirty-fourth Spirit is Furfur. He is a Great and Mighty Earl, appearing in the Form of an Hart with a Fiery Tail. He never speaketh truth unless he be compelled, or brought up within a triangle, Δ. Being therein, he will take upon himself the Form of an Angel. Being bidden, he speaketh with a hoarse voice. Also he will wittingly urge Love between Man and Woman. He can raise Lightnings and Thunders, Blasts, and Great Tempestuous Storms. And he giveth True Answers both of Things Secret and Divine, if commanded. He ruleth over 26 Legions of Spirits. And his Seal is this, etc.

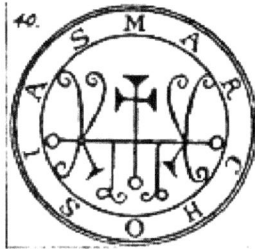

(35.) MARCHOSIAS.

The Thirty-fifth Spirit is Marchosias. He is a Great and Mighty Marquis, appearing at first in the Form of a Wolf 1 having Gryphon's Wings, and a Serpent's Tail, and Vomiting Fire out of his mouth. But after a time, at the command of the Exorcist he putteth on the Shape of a Man. And be is a strong fighter. He was of the Order of Dominations. He governeth 30 Legions of Spirits. He told his Chief, who was Solomon, that after 1,200 years he had hopes to return unto the Seventh Throne. And his Seal is this, to be made and worn as a Lamen, etc.

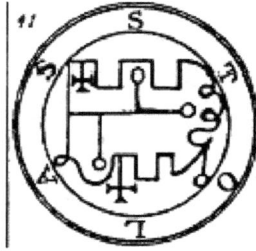

(36.) STOLAS, OR STOLOS.

The Thirty-sixth Spirit is Stolas, or Stolos. He is a Great and Powerful Prince, appearing in the Shape of a Mighty Raven at first before the Exorcist; but after he taketh the image of a Man. He teacheth the Art of Astronomy, and the Virtues of Herbs and Precious Stones. He governeth 26 Legions of Spirits; and his Seal is this, which is, etc.

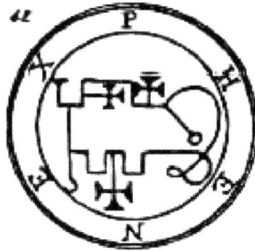

(37.) PHENEX.

The Thirty-Seventh Spirit is Phenex (or Pheynix). He is a great Marquis, and appeareth like the Bird Phoenix, having the Voice of a Child. He singeth many sweet notes before the Exorcist, which he must not regard, but by-and-by he must bid him put on Human Shape. Then he will speak marvellously of all wonderful Sciences if required. He is a Poet, good and excellent. And he will be willing to perform thy requests. He hath hopes also to return to the Seventh Throne after 1,200 years more, as he said unto Solomon. He governeth 20 Legions of Spirits. And his Seal is this, which wear thou, etc.

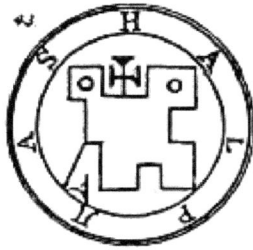

(38.) HALPHAS, OR MALTHUS.

The Thirty-eighth Spirit is Halphas, or Malthous (or Malthas). He is a Great Earl, and appeareth in the Form of a Stock-Dove. He speaketh with a hoarse Voice. His Office is to build up Towers, and to furnish them with Ammunition and Weapons, and to send Men-of-War to places appointed. He ruleth over 26 Legions of Spirits, and his Seal is this, etc.

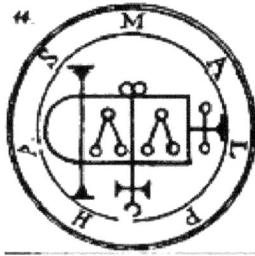

(39.) MALPHAS.

The Thirty-ninth Spirit is Malphas. He appeareth at first like a Crow, but after he will put on Human Shape at the request of the Exorcist, and speak with a hoarse Voice. He is a Mighty President and Powerful. He can build Houses and High Towers, and can bring to thy Knowledge Enemies' Desires and Thoughts, and that which they have done. He giveth Good Familiars. If thou makest a Sacrifice unto him he will receive it kindly and willingly, but he will deceive him that doth it. He governeth 40 Legions of Spirits, and his Seal is this, etc.

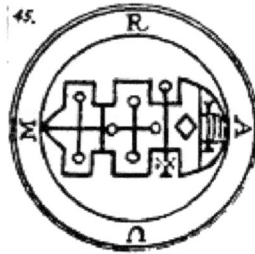

(40.) RAUM.

The Fortieth Spirit is Räum. He is a Great Earl; and appeareth at first in the Form of a Crow, but after the Command of the Exorcist he putteth on Human Shape. His office is to steal Treasures out King's Houses, and to carry it whither he is commanded, and to destroy Cities and Dignities of Men, and to tell all things, Past, and What Is, and what Will Be; and to cause Love between Friends and Foes. He was of the Order of Thrones. He governeth 30 Legions of Spirits; and his Seal is this, which wear thou as aforesaid.

(41.) FOCALOR.

The Forty-first Spirit is Focalor, or Forcalor, or Furcalor. He is a Mighty Duke and Strong. He appeareth in the Form of a Man with Gryphon's Wings. His office is to slay Men, and to drown them in the Waters, and to overthrow Ships of War, for he hath Power over both Winds and Seas; but he will not hurt any man or thing if he be commanded to the contrary by the Exorcist. He also hath hopes to return to the Seventh Throne after 1,000 years. He governeth 30 Legions of Spirits, and his Seal is this, etc.

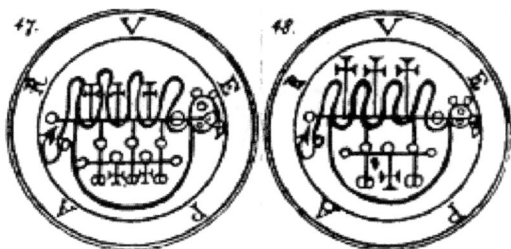

(42.) VEPAR.

The Forty-second Spirit is Vepar, or Vephar. He is a Duke Great and Strong and appeareth like a Mermaid. His office is to govern the Waters, and to guide Ships laden with Arms, Armour, and Ammunition, etc., thereon. And at the request of the Exorcist he can cause the seas to be right stormy and to appear full of ships. Also he maketh men to die in Three Days by Putrefying Wounds or Sores, and causing Worms to breed in them. He governeth 29 Legions of Spirits, and his Seal is this, etc.

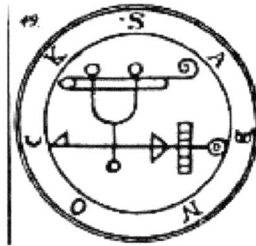

(43.) SABNOCK.

The Forty-third Spirit, as King Solomon commanded them into the Vessel of Brass, is called Sabnock, or Savnok. He is a Marquis, Mighty, Great and Strong, appearing in the Form of an Armed Soldier with a Lion's Head, riding on a pale-coloured horse. His office is to build high Towers, Castles and Cities, and to furnish them with Armour, etc. Also he can afflict Men for many days with Wounds and with Sores rotten and full of Worms. He giveth Good Familiars at the request of the Exorcist. He commandeth 50 Legions of Spirits; and his Seal is this, etc.

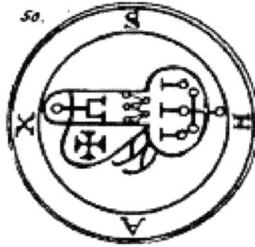

(44.) SHAN.

The Forty-fourth Spirit is Shax, or Shaz (or Shass). He is a Great Marquis and appeareth in the Form of a Stock-Dove, speaking with a voice hoarse, but yet subtle. His Office is to take away the Sight, Hearing, or Understanding of any Man or Woman at the command of the Exorcist; and to steal money out of the houses of Kings, and to carry it again in 1,200 years. If commanded he will fetch Horses at the request of the Exorcist, or any other thing. But he must first be commanded into a Triangle, Δ, or else he will deceive him, and tell him many Lies. He can discover all things that are Hidden, and not kept by Wicked Spirits. He giveth good Familiars, sometimes. He governeth 30 Legions of Spirits, and his Seal is this, etc.

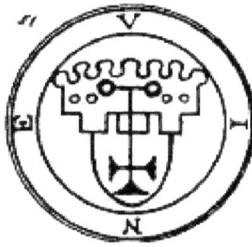

(45.) VINÉ.

The Forty-fifth Spirit is Viné, or Vinea. He is a Great King, and an Earl; and appeareth in the Form of a Lion, 1 riding upon a Black Horse, and bearing a Viper in his hand. His Office is to discover Things Hidden, Witches, Wizards, and Things Present, Past, and to Come. He, at the command of the Exorcist will build Towers, overthrow Great Stone Walls, and make the Waters rough with Storms. He governeth 36 Legions of Spirits. And his Seal is this, which wear thou, as aforesaid, etc.

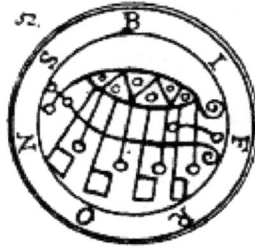

(46.) BIFRONS.

The Forty-sixth Spirit is called Bifrons, or Bifröus, or Bifrovs. He is an Earl, and appeareth in the Form of a Monster; but after a while, at the Command of the Exorcist, he putteth on the shape of a Man. His Office is to make one knowing in Astrology, Geometry, and other Arts and Sciences. He teacheth the Virtues of Precious Stones and Woods. He changeth Dead Bodies, and putteth them in another place; also he lighteth seeming Candles upon the Graves of the Dead. He hath under his Command 6 Legions of Spirits. His Seal is this, which he will own and submit unto, etc.

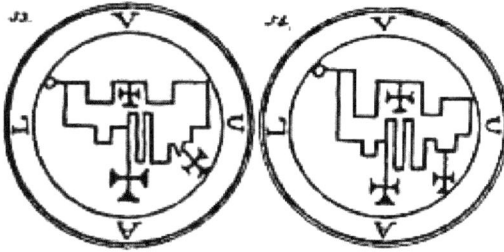

(47.) UVALL, VUAL, OR VOVAL.

The Forty-seventh Spirit Uvall, or Vual, or Voval. He is a Duke, Great, Mighty, and Strong; and appeareth in the Form of a Mighty Dromedary at the first, but after a while at the Command of the Exorcist he putteth on Human Shape, and speaketh the Egyptian Tongue, but not perfectly. 1 His Office is to procure the Love of Woman, and to tell Things Past, Present, and to Come. He also procureth Friendship between Friends and Foes. He was of the Order of Potestates or Powers. He governeth 37 Legions of Spirits, and his Seal is this, to be made and worn before thee, etc.

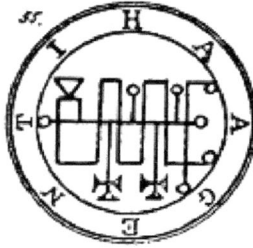

(48.) HAAGENTI.

The Forty-eighth Spirit is Haagenti. He is a President, appearing in the Form of a Mighty Bull with Gryphon's Wings. This is at first, but after, at the Command of the Exorcist he putteth on Human Shape. His Office is to make Men wise, and to instruct them in divers things; also to Transmute all Metals into Gold; and to change Wine into Water, and Water into Wine. He governeth 33 Legions of Spirits, and his Seal is this, etc.

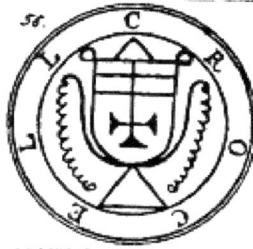

(49.) CROCELL.

The Forty-ninth Spirit is Crocell, or Crokel. He appeareth in the Form of an Angel. He is a Duke Great and Strong, speaking something Mystically of Hidden Things. He teacheth the Art of Geometry and the Liberal Sciences. He, at the Command of the Exorcist, will produce Great Noises like the Rushings of many Waters, although there be none. He warmeth Waters, and discovereth Baths. He was of the Order of Potestates, or Powers, before his fall, as he declared unto the King Solomon. He governeth 48 Legions of Spirits. His Seal is this, that which wear thou as aforesaid.

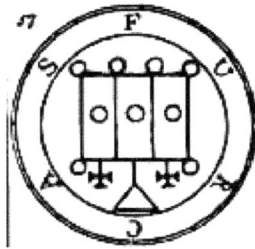

(50.) FURCAS.

The Fiftieth Spirit is Furcas. He is a Knight, and appeareth in the Form of a Cruel Old Man with a long Beard and a hoary Head, riding upon a pale-coloured Horse, with a Sharp Weapon in his hand. His Office is to teach the Arts of Philosophy, Astrology, Rhetoric, Logic, Cheiromancy, and Pyromancy, in all their parts, and perfectly. He hath under his Power 20 Legions of Spirits. His Seal, or Mark, is thus made, etc.

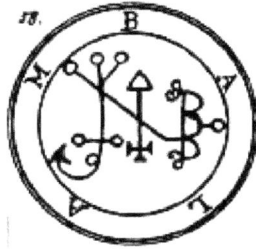

(51.) BALAM.

The Fifty-first Spirit is Balam or Balaam. He is a Terrible, Great, and Powerful King. He appeareth with three Heads: the first is like that of a Bull; the second is like that of a Man; the third is like that of a Ram. He hath the Tail of a Serpent, and Flaming Eyes. He rideth upon a furious Bear, and carrieth a Boshawk upon his Fist. He speaketh with a hoarse Voice, giving True Answers of Things Past, Present, and to Come. He maketh men to go Invisible, and also to be Witty. He governeth 40 Legions of Spirits. His Seal is this, etc.

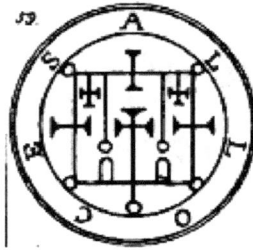

(52.) ALLOCES.

The Fifty-second Spirit is Alloces, or Alocas. He is a Duke, Great, Mighty, and Strong, appearing in the Form of a Soldier 1 riding upon a Great Horse. His Face is like that of a Lion, very Red, and having Flaming Eyes. His Speech is hoarse and very big. 2 His Office is to teach the Art of Astronomy, and all the Liberal Sciences. He bringeth unto thee Good Familiars; also he ruleth over 36 Legions of Spirits. His Seal is this, which, etc.

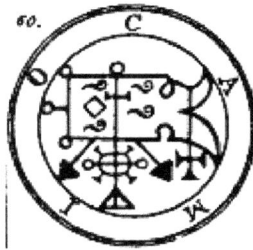

(53.) CAMIO OR CAIM.

The Fifty-third Spirit is Camio, or Caim. He is a Great President, and appeareth in the Form of the Bird called a Thrush at first, but afterwards he putteth on the Shape of a Man carrying in his Hand a Sharp Sword. He seemeth to answer in Burning Ashes, or in Coals of Fire. He is a Good Disputer. His Office is to give unto Men the Understanding of all Birds, Lowing of Bullocks, Barking of Dogs, and other Creatures; and also of the Voice of the Waters. He giveth True Answers of Things to Come. He was of the Order of Angels, but now ruleth over 30 Legions of Spirits Infernal. His Seal is this, which wear thou, etc.

(54.) MURMUR, OR MURMUS.

The Fifty-fourth Spirit is called Murmur, or Murmus, or Murmux. He is a Great Duke, and an Earl; and appeareth in the Form of a Warrior riding upon a Gryphon, with a Ducal Crown upon his Head. There do go before him those his Ministers with great Trumpets sounding. His Office is to teach Philosophy perfectly, and to constrain Souls Deceased to come before the Exorcist to answer those questions which he may wish to put to them, if desired. He was partly of the Order of Thrones, and partly of that of Angels. He now ruleth 30 Legions of Spirits. And his Seal is this, etc.

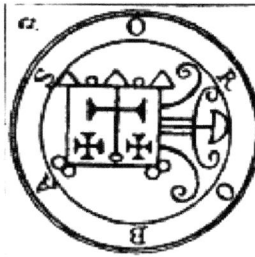

(55.) OROBAS.

The Fifty-fifth Spirit is Orobas. He is a great and Mighty Prince, appearing at first like a Horse; but after the command of the Exorcist he putteth on the Image of a Man. His Office is to discover all things Past, Present, and to Come; also to give Dignities, and Prelacies, and the Favour of Friends and of Foes. He giveth True Answers of Divinity, and of the Creation of the World. He is very faithful unto the Exorcist, and will not suffer him to be tempted of any Spirit. He governeth 20 Legions of Spirits. His Seal is this, etc.

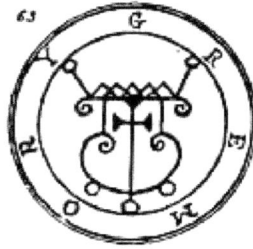

(56) GREMORY, OR GAMORI.

The Fifty-sixth Spirit is Gremory, or Gamori. He is a Duke Strong and Powerful, and appeareth in the Form of a Beautiful Woman, with a Duchess's Crown tied about her waist, and riding on a Great Camel. His Office is to tell of all Things Past, Present, and to Come; and of Treasures Rid, and what they lie in; and to procure the Love of Women both Young and Old. He governeth 26 Legions of Spirits, and his Seal is this, etc.

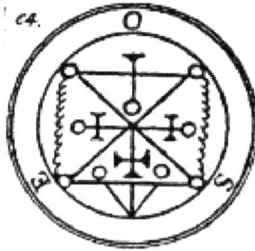

(57.) OSÉ, OR VOSO.

The Fifty-seventh Spirit is Oso, Osé, or Voso. He is a Great President, and appeareth like a Leopard at the first, but after a little time he putteth on the Shape of a Man. His Office is to make one cunning in the Liberal Sciences, and to give True Answers of Divine and Secret Things; also to change a Man into any Shape that the Exorcist pleaseth, so that he that is so changed will not think any other thing than that he is in verity that Creature or Thing he is changed into. He governeth 30 Legions of Spirits, and this is his Seal, etc.

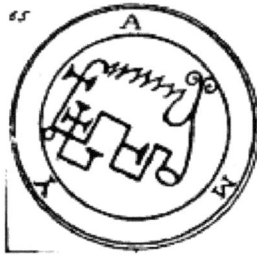

(58.) AMY, OR AVNAS.

The Fifty-eighth Spirit is Amy, or Avnas. He is a Great President, and appeareth at first in the Form of a Flaming Fire; but after a while he putteth on the Shape of a Man. His office is to make one Wonderful Knowing 2 in Astrology and all the Liberal Sciences. He giveth Good Familiars, and can bewray Treasure that is kept by Spirits. He governeth 36 Legions of Spirits, and his Seal is this, etc.

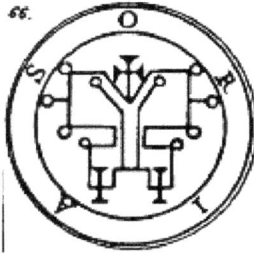

(59.) ORIAX, OR ORIAS.

The Fifty-ninth Spirit is Oriax, or Orias. He is a Great Marquis, and appeareth in the Form of a Lion, 3 riding upon a Horse Mighty and Strong, with a Serpent's Tail; 4 and he holdeth in his Right Hand two Great Serpents hissing. His Office is to teach the Virtues of the Stars, and to know the Mansions of the Planets, and how to understand their Virtues. He also transformeth Men, and he giveth Dignities, Prelacies, and Confirmation thereof; also Favour with Friends and with Foes. He doth govern 30 Legions of Spirits; and his Seal is this, etc.

(60.) VAPULA, OR NAPHULA.

The Sixtieth Spirit is Vapula, or Naphula. He is a Duke Great, Mighty, and Strong; appearing in the Form of a Lion with Gryphon's Wings. His Office is to make Men Knowing in all Handcrafts and Professions, also in Philosophy, and other Sciences. He governeth 36 Legions of Spirits, and his Seal or Character is thus made, and thou shalt wear it as aforesaid, etc.

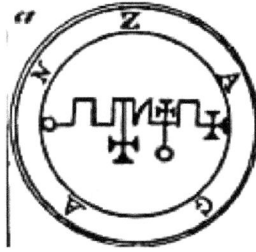

(61.) ZAGAN.

The Sixty-first Spirit is Zagan. He is a Great King and President, appearing at first in the Form of a Bull with Gryphon's Wings; but after a while he putteth on Human Shape. He maketh Men Witty. He can turn Wine into Water, and Blood into Wine, also Water into Wine. He can turn all Metals into Coin of the Dominion that Metal is of. He can even make Fools wise. He governeth 33 Legions of Spirits, and his Seal is this, etc.

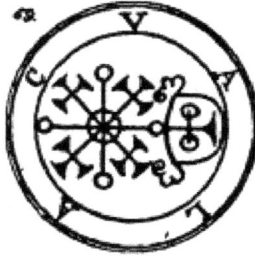

(62.) VOLAC, OR VALAX, OR VALU, OR UALAC.

The Sixty-second Spirit is Volac, or Valak, or Valu. He is a President Mighty and Great, and appeareth like a Child with Angel's Wings, riding on a Two-headed Dragon. His Office is to give True Answers of Hidden Treasures, and to tell where Serpents may be seen. The which he will bring unto the Exorciser without any Force or Strength being by him employed. He governeth 38 Legions of Spirits, and his Seal is thus.

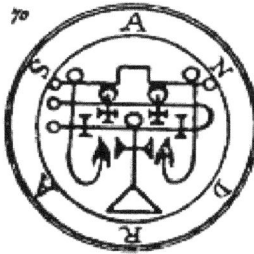

(63.) ANDRAS.

The Sixty-third Spirit is Andras. He is a Great Marquis, appearing in the Form of an Angel with a Head like a Black Night Raven, riding upon a strong Black Wolf, and having a Sharp and Bright Sword flourished aloft in his hand. His Office is to sow Discords. If the Exorcist have not a care, he will slay both him and his fellows. He governeth 30 Legions of Spirits, and this is his Seal, etc.

(64.) HAURES, OR HAURAS, OR HAVRES, OR FLAUROS.

The Sixty-fourth Spirit is Haures, or Hauras, or Havres, or Flauros. He is a Great Duke, and appeareth at first like a Leopard, Mighty, Terrible, and Strong, but after a while, at the Command of the Exorcist, he putteth on Human Shape with Eyes Flaming and Fiery, and a most Terrible Countenance. He giveth True Answers of all things, Present, Past, and to Come. But if he be not commanded into a Triangle, △, he will Lie in all these Things, and deceive and beguile the Exorcist in these things, or in such and such business. He will, lastly, talk of the Creation of the World, and of Divinity, and of how he and other Spirits fell. He destroyeth and burneth up those who be the Enemies of the Exorcist should he so desire it; also he will not suffer him to be tempted by any other Spirit or otherwise. He governeth 36 Legions of Spirits, and his Seal is this, to be worn as a Lamen, etc.

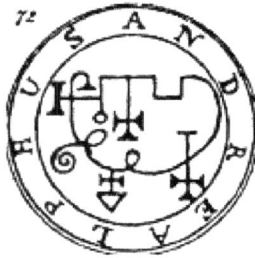

(65.) ANDREALPHUS.

The Sixty-fifth Spirit is Andrealphus. He is a Mighty Marquis, appearing at first in the form of a Peacock, with great Noises. But after a time he putteth on Human shape. He can teach Geometry perfectly. He maketh Men very subtle therein; and in all Things pertaining unto Mensuration or Astronomy. He can transform a Man into the Likeness of a Bird. He governeth 30 Legions of Infernal Spirits, and his Seal is this, etc.

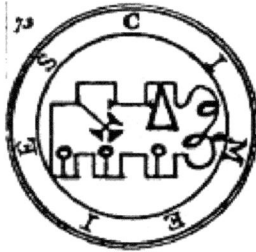

(66.) CIMEJES, OR CIMEIES, OR KIMARIS.

The Sixty-sixth Spirit is Cimejes, or Cimeies, or Kimaris. He is a Marquis, Mighty, Great, Strong and Powerful, appearing like a Valiant Warrior riding upon a goodly Black Horse. He ruleth over all Spirits in the parts of Africa. His Office is to teach perfectly Grammar, Logic, Rhetoric, and to discover things Lost or Hidden, and Treasures. He governeth 20 Legions of Infernals; and his Seal is this, etc.

(67.) AMDUSIAS, OR AMDUKIAS.

The Sixty-seventh Spirit is Amdusias, or Amdukias. He is a Duke
Great and Strong, appearing at first like a Unicorn, but at the
request of the Exorcist he standeth before him in Human Shape,
causing Trumpets, and all manner of Musical Instruments to be
heard, but not soon or immediately. Also he can cause Trees to
bend and incline according to the Exorcist's Will. He giveth
Excellent Familiars. He governeth 29 Legions of Spirits. And his
Seal is this, etc.

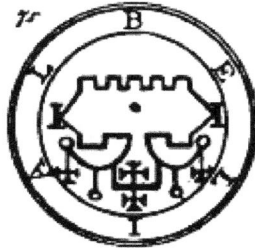

(68.) BELIAL.

The Sixty-eighth Spirit is Belial. He is a Mighty and a Powerful King, and was created next after LUCIFER. He appeareth in the Form of Two Beautiful Angels sitting in a Chariot of Fire. He speaketh with a Comely Voice, and declareth that he fell first from among the worthier sort, that were before Michael, and other Heavenly Angels. His Office is to distribute Presentations and Senatorships, etc.; and to cause favour of Friends and of Foes. He giveth excellent Familiars, and governeth 50 Legions of Spirits. Note well that this King Belial. must have Offerings, Sacrifices and Gifts presented unto him by the Exorcist, or else he will not give True Answers unto his Demands. But then he tarrieth not one hour in the Truth, unless he be con. strained by Divine Power. And his Seal is this, which is to be worn as aforesaid, etc.

(69.) DECARABIA.

The Sixty-ninth Spirit is Decarabia. He appeareth in the Form of a Star in a Pentacle, at first; but after, at the command of the Exorcist, he putteth on the image of a Man. His Office is to discover the Virtues of Birds and Precious Stones, and to make the Similitude of all kinds of Birds to fly before the Exorcist, singing and drinking as natural Birds do. He governeth 30 Legions of Spirits, being himself a Great Marquis. And this is his Seal, which is to be worn, etc.

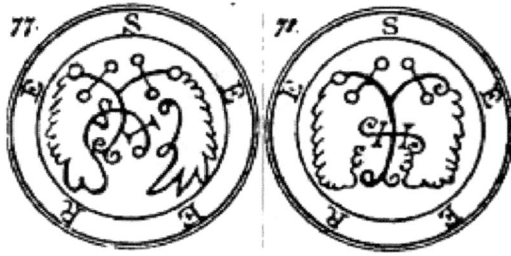

(70.) SEERE, SEAR, OR SEIR.

The Seventieth Spirit is Seere, Sear, or Seir. He is a Mighty Prince, and Powerful, under AMAYMON, King of the East. He appeareth in the Form of a Beautiful Man, riding upon a Winged Horse. His Office is to go and come; and to bring abundance of things to pass on a sudden, and to carry or recarry anything whither thou wouldest have it to go, or whence thou wouldest have it from. He can pass over the whole Earth in the twinkling of an Eye. He giveth a True relation of all sorts of Theft, and of Treasure hid, and of many other things. He is of an indifferent Good Nature, and is willing to do anything which the Exorcist desireth. He governeth 26 Legions of Spirits. And this his Seal is to be worn, etc.

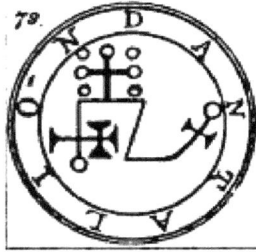

(71.) DANTALION.

The Seventy-first Spirit is Dantalion. He is a Duke Great and Mighty, appearing in the Form of a Man with many Countenances, all Men's and Women's Faces; and he hath a Book in his right hand. His Office is to teach all Arts and Sciences unto any; and to declare the Secret Counsel of any one; for he knoweth the Thoughts of all Men and Women, and can change them at his Will. He can cause Love, and show the Similitude of any person, and show the same by a Vision, let them be in what part of the World they Will. He governeth 36 Legions of Spirits; and this is his Seal, which wear thou, etc.

(72.) ANDROMALIUS.

The Seventy-second Spirit in Order is named Andromalius. He is an Earl, Great and Mighty, appearing in the Form of a Man holding a Great Serpent in his Hand. His Office is to bring back both a Thief, and the Goods which be stolen; and to discover all Wickedness, and Underhand Dealing; and to punish all Thieves and other Wicked People and also to discover Treasures that be Hid. He ruleth over 36 Legions of Spirits. His Seal is this, the which wear thou as aforesaid, etc.

These be the 72 Mighty Kings and Princes which King Solomon Commanded into a Vessel of Brass, together with their Legions. Of whom BELIAL, BILETH, ASMODAY, and GAAP, were Chief. And it is to be noted that Solomon did this because of their pride, for he never declared other reason why he thus bound them. And when he had thus bound them up and sealed the Vessel, he by Divine Power did chase them all into a deep Lake or Hole in Babylon. And they of Babylon, wondering to see such a thing, they did then go wholly into the Lake, to break the Vessel open, expecting to find great store of Treasure therein. But when they had broken it open, out flew the Chief Spirits immediately, with their Legions following them; and they were all restored to their former places except BELIAL, who entered into a certain Image, and thence gave answers unto those who did offer Sacrifices unto him, and did worship the Image as their God, etc.

OBSERVATIONS

FIRST, thou shalt know and observe the Moon's Age for thy working. The best days be when the Moon Luna is 2, 4, 6, 8, 10, 12, or 14 days old, as Solomon saith; and no other days be profitable. The Seals of the 72 Kings are to be made in Metals. The Chief Kings' in Sol (Gold); Marquises' in Luna (Silver); Dukes' in Venus (Copper); Prelacies' in Jupiter (Tin); Knights' in Saturn (Lead) Presidents' in Mercury (Mercury); Earls' in Venus (Copper), and Luna (Silver), alike equal, etc. THESE 72 Kings be under the Power of AMAYMON, CORSON, ZIMIMAY or ZIMINAIR, and GÖAP, who are the Four Great Kings ruling in the Four Quarters, or Cardinal Points, viz.: East, West, North, and South, and are not to be called forth except it be upon Great Occasions; but are to be Invocated and Commanded to send such or such a Spirit that is under their Power and Rule, as is shown in the following Invocations or Conjurations. And the Chief Kings may be bound from 9 till 12 o'clock at Noon, and from 3 till Sunset; Marquises may be bound from 3 in the afternoon till 9 at Night, and from 9 at Night till Sunrise; Dukes may be bound from Sunrise till Noonday in Clear Weather; Prelates may be bound any hour of the Day; Knights may from Dawning of Day till Sunrise, or from 4 o'clock till Sunset; Presidents may be bound any time, excepting Twilight, at Night, unless the King whom they are under be Invocated; and Counties or Earls any hour of the Day, so it be in Woods, or in any other places whither men resort not, or where no noise is, etc.

CLASSIFIED LIST OF THE 72 CHIEF SPIRITS OF THE GOETIA, ACCORDING TO RESPECTIVE RANK.

(Seal in Gold.) KINGS.--(1.) Bael; (9.) Paimon; (13.) Beleth; (20.) Purson; (32.) Asmoday; (45.) Viné; (51.) Balam; (61.) Zagan; (68.) Belial.

(Seal in Copper.) DUKES.--(2.) Agares; (6.) Valefor; (8.) Barbatos; (11.) Gusion;(15.) Eligos; (16.) Zepar; (18.) Bathim; (19.) Sallos; (23.) Aim; (26.) Buné; (28.) Berith; (29.) Astaroth; (41.) Focalor; (42.) Vepar; (47.) Vual; (49.) Crocell; (52.) Alloces; (54.) Murmur; (56.) Gremory; (60.) Vapula; (64.) Haures; (67.) Amdusias; (71.) Dantalion.

(Seal in Tin.) PRINCES AND PRELATES.--(3.) Vassago; (12.) Sitri; (22.) Ipos; (33.) Gäap; (36.) Stolas; (55.) Orobas; (70.) Seere.

(Seal in Silver.) MARQUISES.--(4.) Samigina; (7.) Amon; (14.) Leraje; (24.) Naberius; (27.) Ronové; (30.) Forneus; (35.) Marchosias; (37.) Phenex; (43.) Sabnock; (44.) Shax; (59.) Orias; (63.) Andras; (65.) Andrealphus; (66.) Cimeies; (69.) Decarabia.

(Seal in Mercury.) PRESIDENTS.-- (5.) Marbas; (10.) Buer; (17.) Botis; (21.) Marax; (25.) Glasya-Labolas; (31.) Foras; (33.) Gäap; (39.) Malphas; (48.) Häagenti; (53.) Caim; (57.) Ose; (58.) Amy; (61.) Zagan; (62.) Valac.

(Seal in Copper and Silver alike equal.) EARLS, or COUNTS.--(17.) Botis; (21.) Marax; (25.) Glasya-Labolas; (27.) Ronové; (34.) Furfur; (38.) Halphas; (40.) Räum; (45.) Viné; (46.) Bifrons; (72.) Andromalius.

(Seal in Lead.) KNIGHTS.--(50.) Furcas.

1. Bael בָּאֶל Figure 81.	2. Agares אַנאַראַש Figure 82.	3. Vassago וְשַׁאֲנוּ Figure 83.	4. Gamigin נאָמִינן Figure 84.	5. Marbas מארבש Figure 85.	6. Valefor וַאֲלְפָאר Figure 86.
7. Amon אָמוֹן Figure 87.	8. Barbatos. בּרבטוֹש Figure 88.	9. Paimon פּאִימוֹן Figure 89.	10. Buer. בּוֹאֶר Figure 90.	11 Gusion. גוּסִיוֹן Figure 91.	12. Sitri. שִׁיטרִי Figure 92.
13. Beleth. בְּלָאֶת Figure 93	14. Leraje לְרַאיךְ Figure 94.	15. Eligos. אֶלִיגוֹש Figure 95.	16 Zepar. זאֶפַר Figure 96.	17. Botis בּוֹטִיש Figure 97.	18. Bathin. בַּאתִין Figure 98.
19. Sallos. שַׁאֲלוֹש Figure 99.	20. Purson. פּוּרְשׁוֹן Figure 100	21. Marax. מַארַאֶס Figure 101.	22 Ipos יְפוֹש Figure 102.	23. Aim. אִים Figure 103.	24 Naberius. נַבְּרִיוֹש Figure 104.
Glaya-Labolas נלאֶסֲאֶ־לֶב ־וּלֶשׁ Figure 105	26. Bime. בִּים Figure 106.	27. Ronove. רוֹנוֹן Figure 107	28. Berith. בְּרִית Figure 108.	29. Astaroth. אֶשׁטַארוֹת Figure 109.	30. Forneus פֶהוֹרנאֶוֹש Figure 110
31. Foras פּוֹראַש Figure 111.	32. Asmoday אֶסטוֹדִי Figure 112	33. Gaap. נאַאֶף Figure 113.	34. Furfur. פֶהוּרפֶהוּר Figure 114	35. Marchosias מַרחוֹשִׁיאַש Figure 115.	36 Stolas. שטוֹלוֹש Figure 116
37. Phenex פּאֶנִיס Figure 117.	38. Malthas מאַלתש Figure 118.	39. Malphas מאַלפַּש Figure 119.	40. Raum. ראוֹם Figure 120.	41. Focalor. פֶהוֹרקלוֹר Figure 121.	42. Vepar וּפֶאַר Figure 122
43 Sabnock שְׁבְּנוֹךְ Figure 123.	44 Shax. שַׁאֶז Figure 124.	45. Vine. וִינאֶ Figure 125	46 Bifrons. בִּיפֶהרוֹנש Figure 126	47. Uvall. ווַאֶל Figure 127	48. Haagenti הָאַננטִי Figure 128.
49 Crocell. כּרוֹכֶל Figure 129.	50 Furcas פֶהֹחַכש Figure 130.	51. Balam. בַּאלאַם Figure 131	52. Alloces. אֶלוֹכאַש Figure 132.	53. Camio. כַּאמִיוֹ Figure 133.	54 Murmus מוֹרמוֹס Figure 134
55. Orobas וּרוֹבַש Figure 135.	56. Gamori נְמוֹרִי Figure 136	57. Voso וֹשׁוֹ Figure 137.	58. Avnas אוֹנַש Figure 138	59. Oriax וֹרִיאַס Figure 139.	60. Naphula נְפוֹלאַ Figure 140
61 Zagan זאַנאַן Figure 141.	62 Valu וַאֲלוּ Figure 142	63 Andras אַנדראַש Figure 143	64 Haures. הַאוֹראֶש Figure 144.	Andrealphus אַנדראַלפֶהה־ רֶשׁ Figure 145	66. Kimaris. כִּימַארִיש Figure 146.
Amdukias אַמדוֹכִיאַש Figure 147	68. Belial בּלִיאַל Figure 148	Decarobia דְכַארבִּיאַ Figure 149.	70. Seere שַׁאֶר Figure 150.	Dantalion. ראַנטַאלִיוֹן Figure 151.	Andromalius אַנדרוֹכּלִי־ וֹשׁ Figure 152.

99

THE MAGICAL CIRCLE

This is the Form of the Magical Circle of King Solomon, the which he made that he might preserve himself therein from the malice of these Evil Spirits. (See Frontispiece, Figure 153) This Magical Circle is to be made 9 feet across, and the Divine Names are to be written around it, beginning at EHYEH, and ending at LEVANAH, Luna.

(Colours.--The space between the outer and inner circles, where the serpent is coiled, with the Hebrew names written along his body, is bright deep yellow. The square in the centre of the circle, where the word "Master" is written, is filled in with red. All names and letters are in black. In the Hexagrams the outer triangles where the letters A, D, O, N, A, I, appear are filled in with bright yellow, the centres, where the T-shaped crosses are, blue or green. In the Pentagrams outside the circle, the outer triangles where "Te, tra, gram, ma, ton," is written, are filled in bright yellow, and the centres with the T crosses written therein are red.)

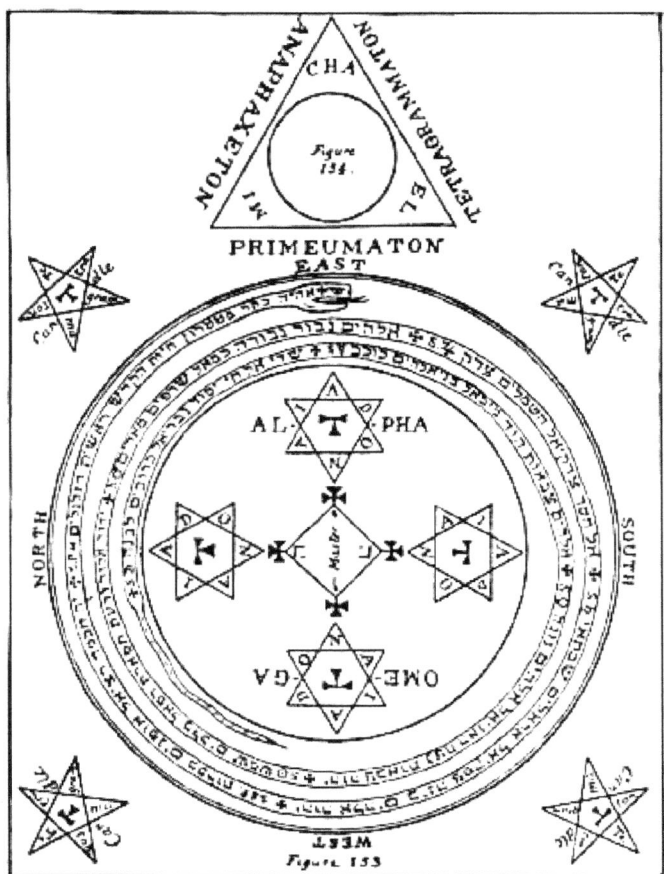

Figure 153

Figure 154.

THE MAGICAL TRIANGLE OF SOLOMON

This is the Form of the Magical Triangle, into the which Solomon did command the Evil Spirits. It is to be made at 2 feet distance from the Magical Circle and it is 3 feet across. (See Frontispiece Figure 154.) Note that this triangle is to be placed toward that quarter whereunto the Spirit belongeth. And the base of the triangle is to be nearest unto the Circle, the apex pointing in the direction of the quarter of the Spirit. Observe thou also the Moon in thy working, as aforesaid, etc. Anaphaxeton is sometimes written Anepheneton.

(Colours.--Triangle outlined in black; name of Michael black on white ground; the three Names without the triangle written in red; circle in centre entirely filled in in dark green.)

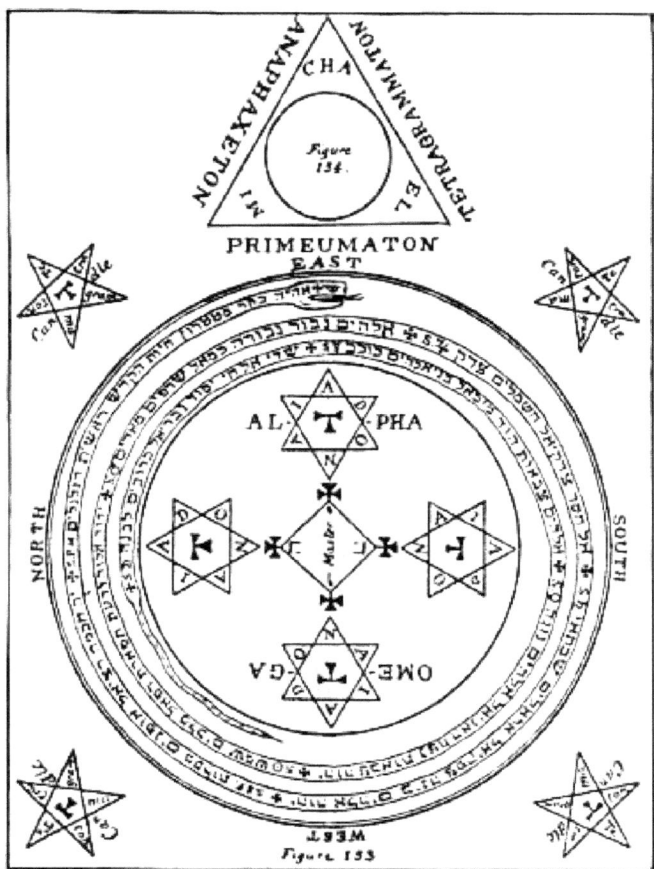

CHA

ANAPHAXETON

TETRAGRAMMATON

MI

EL

Figure 154.

PRIMEUMATON
EAST

Consile

Consile

AL·PHA

NORTH

SOUTH

Master

OME·GA

Consile

Consile

WEST
Figure 153

103

THE HEXAGRAM OF SOLOMON

THIS is the Form of the Hexagram of Solomon, the figure whereof is to be made on parchment of a calf's skin, and worn at the skirt of thy white vestment, and covered with a cloth of fine linen white and pure, the which is to be shown unto the Spirits when they do appear, so that they be compelled to take human shape upon them and be obedient.

(Colours.--Circle, Hexagon, and T cross in centre outlined in black, Maltese crosses black; the five exterior triangles of the Hexagram where Te, tra, gram, ma, ton, is written, are filled in with bright yellow; the T cross in centre is red, with the three little squares therein in black. The lower exterior triangle, where the Sigil is drawn in black, is left white. The words "Tetragrammaton" and "Tau" are in black letters; and AGLA with Alpha and Omega in red letters.)

THE PENTAGRAM OF SOLOMON

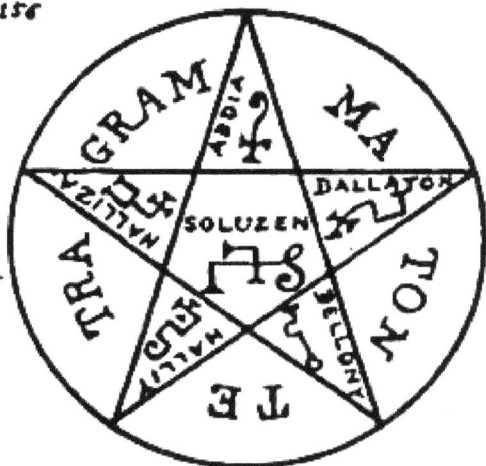

THIS is the Form of Pentagram of Solomon, the figure whereof is to be made in Sol or Luna (Gold or Silver), and worn upon thy breast; having the Seal of the Spirit required upon the other side thereof. It is to preserve thee from danger, and also to command the Spirits by.

(Colours.--Circle and pentagram outlined in black. Names and Sigils within Pentagram black also. "Tetragrammaton" in red letters. Ground of centre of Pentagram, where "Soluzen" is written, green. External angles of Pentagram where "Abdia", "Ballaton," "Halliza," etc., are written, blue.)

THE MAGIC RING OR DISC OF SOLOMON

THIS is the Form of the Magic Ring, or rather Disc, of Solomon, the figure whereof is to be made in gold or silver. It is to be held before the face of the exorcist to preserve him from the stinking sulphurous fumes and flaming breath of the Evil Spirits.

(Colour.--Bright yellow. Letters, black.)

THE VESSEL OF BRASS

THIS is the Form of the Vessel of Brass wherein King Solomon did shut up the Evil Spirits, etc. (See Figures 158 and 159.) (Somewhat different forms are given in the various codices. The seal in Figure 160 was made in brass to cover this vessel with at the top. This history of the genii shut up in the brazen vessel by King Solomon recalls the story of "The Fisherman and the Jinni" in "The Arabian Nights." In this tale, however, there was only one jinni shut up in a vessel of yellow brass the which was covered at the top with a leaden seal. This jinni tells the fisherman that his name is Sakhr, or Sacar.)

(Colour.--Bronze. Letters.--Black on a red band.)

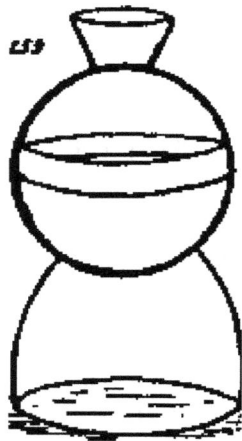

THE SECRET SEAL OF SOLOMON

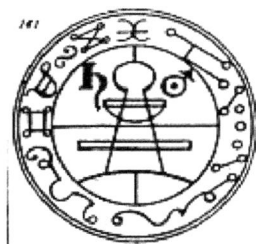

THIS is the Form of the Secret Seal of Solomon, wherewith he did bind and seal up the aforesaid Spirits with their legions in the Vessel of Brass.

This seal is to be made by one that is clean both inwardly and outwardly, and that hath not defiled himself by any woman in the space of a month, but hath in prayer and fasting desired of God to forgive him all his sins, etc.

It is to be made on the day of Mars or Saturn (Tuesday or Saturday) at night at 12 o'clock, and written upon virgin parchment with the blood of a black cock that never trode hen. Note that on this night the moon must be increasing in light (i.e., going from new to full) and in the Zodiacal Sign of Virgo. And when the seal is so made thou shalt perfume it with alum, raisins dried in the sun, dates, cedar and lignum aloes.

Also, by this seal King Solomon did command all the aforesaid Spirits in the Vessel of Brass, and did seal it up with this same seal. He by it gained the love of all manner of persons, and overcame in battle, for neither weapons, nor fire, nor water could hurt him. And this privy seal was made to cover the vessel at the top withal, etc.

Note: Figures 162 to 174 inclusive are interesting as showing a marked resemblance to the central design of the Secret Seal. It will be observed that the evident desire is to represent hieroglyphically a person raising his or her hands in adoration. Nearly all are stone sepulchral steles, and the execution of them is rough and primitive in the extreme. Most are in the Musëe du Louvre at Paris.

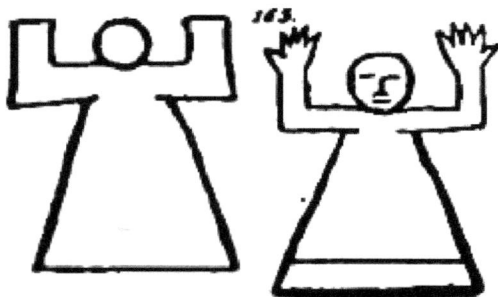

162.

163.

Figures 162 and 163 are from the district of Constantine and show a figure raising its arms in adoration.

164.

In Figure 164 , also from Constantine, the person bears a palm branch in the right hand. Above is a hieroglyphic representing either the Lunar Disc or the Sun in the heavens; but more probably the former.

Figure 165 is a more complicated stele. Above is the symbol already mentioned, then comes the sign of the Pentagram, represented by a five-pointed star, towards which the person raises his or her hands. Besides the latter is a rude form of caduceus. A brief inscription follows in the Punic character. The Punic or Carthaginian language is usually considered to have been a dialect. of Phœnician, and Carthage was of course a colony of Tyre. Beneath the Tunic inscription is a horse's head in better drawing than the sculpture of the rest of the stele, which would seem to imply that the rudeness of the representation of the human figure is intentional. This and the following stele are also from Constantine.

In Figure 166 again, the horse is best delineated by far. In addition to the other symbols there is either a hand or a foot, for it is almost impossible to distinguish which, at the head of the stele, followed by an egg-and-tongue moulding. The figure of the person with the arms raised is treated as a pure hieroglyphic and is placed between two rude caducei. The Lunar or Solar Symbol follows.

Figure 167, also from Constantine, shows the last-mentioned symbol above. The figure with the arms raised is simply a hieroglyph, and is placed between an arm and hand on the one side, and a rude caduceus on the other.

168.

Figure 168 shows the person holding a rude caduceus in the right hand, and standing above a dolphin. This latter, as in the case of the horse in 165 and 166, is by far the best delineated.

169.

Figure 169, this also being from Constantine, shows the usual human hieroglyph between a caduceus and a crescent.

170.

Figure 170 is from the site of ancient Carthage. It is very rough in workmanship, and the designs are mere scratchings on the stone. The ensemble has the effect of an evil Sigil.

171.

Figure 171 is also from Carthage and the various symbols appear to have become compressed into and synthesised in the form of a peculiarly evil-looking caduceus.

172.

Figure 172 is from the decoration of a sepulchral urn found at Oldenburgh in Germany. It is remarkable as showing the same hieroglyphic human form with the crescent above; the latter in the Secret Seal of Solomon has a flattened top, and is therefore more like a bowl, and is placed across the hieroglyph.

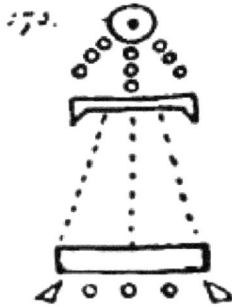

Figure 173 is an Egyptian design which would show an analogy between the symbol and the idea of the force of the creation.

Figure 174 is a stele from Phœnicia somewhat similar to the others, except that the rudimentary caducei in Figures 166 and 170 are here replaced by two roughly drawn Ionic columns.

These last three designs are taken from the work of the Chevalier Emile Soldi-Colbert de Beaulieu, on the "Langue Sacrée."

In Figure 175 is given the Seal of the Spirit HALAHEL. This Spirit is said to be under the rule of BAEL, and to be of a mixed nature, partly good and partly evil, like the spirits of Theurgia-Goetia which follow in the second book of the Lemegeton.

115

THE OTHER MAGICAL REQUISITES

THE other magical requisites are: a sceptre, a sword, a mitre, a cap, a long white robe of linen, and other garments for the purpose; also a girdle of lion's skin three inches broad, with all the names written about it which he round the outmost part of the Magical Circle. Also perfumes, and a chafing-dish of charcoal kindled to put the fumes on, to smoke or perfume the place appointed for action; also anointing oil to anoint thy temples and thine eyes with; and fair water to wash thyself in. And in so doing, thou shalt say as David said:

THE ADORATION AT THE BATH

"Thou shalt purge me with hyssop, O Lord! and I shall be clean: Thou shalt wash me, and I shall be whiter than snow."

And at the putting on of thy garments thou shalt say: THE ADORATION AT THE INDUING OF THE VESTMENTS.

"By the figurative mystery of these holy vestures (or of this holy vestment) I will clothe me with the armour of salvation in the strength of the Most High, ANCHOR; AMACOR; AMIDES; THEODINIAS; ANITOR; that my desired end may be effected through Thy strength, O ADONAI! unto Whom the praise and glory will for ever and ever belong! Amen!"

After thou hast so done, make prayers unto God according unto thy work, as Solomon hath commanded.

THE CONJURATION TO CALL FORTH ANY OF THE AFORESAID SPIRITS

I DO invoke and conjure thee, O Spirit, N. 1; and being with power armed from the SUPREME MAJESTY, I do strongly command thee, by BERALANENSIS, BALDACHIENSIS, PAUMACHIA, and APOLOGIAE SEDES; by the most Powerful Princes, Genii, Liachidæ, and Ministers of the Tartarean Abode; and by the Chief Prince of the Seat of Apologia in the Ninth Legion, I do invoke thee, and by invocating conjure thee. And being armed with power from the SUPREME MAJESTY, I do strongly command thee, by Him Who spake and it was done, and unto whom all creatures be obedient. Also I, being made after the image of GOD, endued with power from GOD and created according unto His will, do exorcise thee by that most mighty and powerful name of GOD, EL, strong and wonderful; O thou Spirit N. And I command thee and Him who spake the Word and His FIAT was accomplished, and by all the names of God. Also by the names ADONAI, EL, ELOHIM, ELOHI, EHYEH, ASHER EHYEH, ZABAOTH, ELION, IAH, TETRAGRAMMATON, SHADDAI, LORD GOD MOST HIGH, I do exorcise thee and do powerfully command thee, O thou Spirit N., that thou dost forthwith appear unto me here before this Circle in a fair human shape, without any deformity or tortuosity. And by this ineffable name, TETRAGRAMMATON IEHOVAH, do I command thee, at the which being heard the elements are overthrown, the air is shaken, the sea runneth back, the fire is quenched, the earth trembleth, and all the hosts of the celestials, terrestrials, and infernals, do tremble together, and are troubled and confounded. Wherefore come thou, O Spirit N., forthwith, and without delay, from any or all parts of the world wherever thou mayest be, and make rational answers unto all things that I shall demand of thee. Come thou peaceably, visibly, and affably, now, and without delay, manifesting that which I shall desire. For thou art conjured by the name of the LIVING and TRUE GOD, HELIOREN, wherefore fulfil thou my commands, and persist thou therein unto the end, and according unto mine interest, visibly and affably speaking unto me with a voice clear and intelligible without any ambiguity.

REPEAT this conjuration as often as thou pleasest, and if the Spirit come not yet, say as followeth:

THE SECOND CONJURATION

I DO invoke, conjure, and command thee, O thou Spirit N., to appear and to show thyself visibly unto me before this Circle in fair and comely shape, without any deformity or tortuosity; by the name and in the name IAH and VAU, which Adam heard and spake; and by the name Of GOD, AGLA, which Lot heard and was saved with his family; and by the name IOTH, which Jacob heard from the angel wrestling with him, and was delivered from the hand of Esau his brother; and by the name ANAPHAXETON which Aaron heard and spake and was made wise; and by the name ZABAOTH, which Moses named and all the rivers were turned into blood; and by the name ASHER EHYEH ORISTON, which Moses named, and all the rivers brought forth frogs, and they ascended into the houses, destroying all things; and by the name ELION, which Moses named, and there was great hail such as had not been since the beginning of the world; and by the name ADONAI, which Moses named, and there came up locusts, which appeared upon the whole land, and devoured all which the hail had left; and by the name SCHEMA AMATHIA which Ioshua called upon, and the sun stayed his course; and by the name ALPHA and OMEGA, which Daniel named, and destroyed Bel, and slew the Dragon; and in the name EMMANUEL, which the three children, Shadrach, Meshach and Abed-nego, sang in the midst of the fiery furnace, and were delivered; and by the name HAGIOS; and by the SEAL OF ADONI; and by ISCHYROS, ATHANATOS, PARACLETOS; and by O THEOS, ICTROS, ATHANATOS; and by these three secret names, AGLA, ON, TETRAGRAMMATON, do I adjure and constrain thee. And by these names, and by all the other names of the LIVING and TRUE GOD, the LORD ALMIGHTY, I do exorcise and command thee, O Spirit N., even by Him Who spake the Word and it was done, and to Whom all creatures are obedient; and by the dreadful judgments of GOD; and by the uncertain Sea of Glass, which is before the DIVINE MAJESTY, mighty and powerful; by the four beasts before the throne, having eyes before and behind; by the fire round about the throne; by the holy angels of Heaven; and by the mighty wisdom of GOD; I do potently exorcise thee, that thou appearest here before this Circle, to fulfil my will in all things which shall seem good unto me; by the Seal of BASDATHEA BALDACHIA; and by this name PRIMEUMATON, which Moses named, and the earth opened, and did swallow up Kora, Dathan, and Abiram. Wherefore thou shalt make faithful answers unto all my demands, O Spirit N., and shalt perform all my desires so far as in thine office thou art capable hereof. Wherefore, come thou, visibly, peaceably, and affably, now without delay, to manifest that which I desire, speaking with a clear and perfect voice, intelligibly, and to mine understanding.

IF HE come not yet at the rehearsal of these two first conjurations (but without doubt he will), say on as followeth; it being a constraint:

THE CONSTRAINT

I Do conjure thee, O thou Spirit N., by all the most glorious and efficacious names of the MOST GREAT AND INCOMPREHENSIBLE LORD GOD op HOSTS, that thou comest quickly and without delay from all parts and places of the earth and world wherever thou mayest be, to make rational answers unto my demands, and that visibly and affably, speaking with a voice intelligible unto mine understanding as aforesaid. I conjure and constrain thee, O thou Spirit N., by all the names aforesaid; and in addition by these seven great names wherewith Solomon the Wise bound thee and thy companions in a Vessel of Brass, ADONAI, PREYAI or PRERAI, TETRAGRAMMATON, ANAPHAXETON or ANEPHENETON, INESSENFATOAL or INESSENFATALL, PATHTUMON or PATHATUMON, and ITEMON; that thou appearest, here before this Circle to fulfil my will in all things that seem good unto me. And if thou be still so disobedient, and refusest still to come, I will in the power and by the power of the name of the SUPREME AND EVERLASTING LORD GOD WHO created both thee and me and all the world in six days, and what is contained therein, EIE, SARAYE, and by the power of this name PRIMEUMATON which commandeth the whole host of Heaven, curse thee, and deprive thee of thine office, joy, and place, and bind thee in the depths of the Bottomless Pit or Abyss, there to remain unto the Day of the Last Judgment. And I will bind thee in the Eternal Fire, and into the Lake of Flame and of Brimstone, unless thou comest quickly and appearest here before this Circle to do my will. Therefore, come thou! in and by the holy names ADONAI, ZABAOTH, ADONAI, AMIORAN. Come thou! for it is ADONAI who commandest thee.

IF THOU hast come thus far, and yet he appeareth not, thou mayest be sure that he is sent unto some other place by his King, and cannot come; and if it be so, invocate the King as here followeth, to send him. But if he do not come still, then thou mayest be sure that he is bound in chains in hell, and that he is not in the custody of his King. If so, and thou still hast a desire to call him even from thence, thou must rehearse the general curse which is called the Spirits' Chain.

Here followeth, therefore, the Invocation of the King:

THE INVOCATION OF THE KING

O THOU great, powerful, and mighty KING AMAIMON, who bearest rule by the power of the SUPREME GOD EL over all spirits both superior and inferior of the Infernal Orders in the Dominion of the East; I do invoke and command thee by the especial and true name Of GOD; and by that God that Thou Worshippest; and by the Seal of thy creation; and by the most mighty and powerful name Of GOD, IEHOVAH TETRAGRAMMATON who cast thee out of heaven with all other infernal spirits; and by all the most powerful and great names of GOD who created Heaven, and Earth, and Hell, and all things in them contained; and by their power and virtue; and by the name PRIMEUMATON who commandeth the whole host of Heaven; that thou mayest cause, enforce, and compel the Spirit N. to come unto me here before this Circle in a fair and comely shape, without harm unto me or unto any other creature, to answer truly and faithfully unto all my requests; so that I may accomplish my will and desire in knowing or obtaining any matter or thing which by office thou knowest is proper for him to perform or accomplish, through the power of GOD, EL, Who created and doth dispose of all things both celestial, aërial, terrestrial, and infernal.

AFTER thou shalt have invoked the King in this manner twice or thrice over, then conjure the spirit thou wouldst call forth by the aforesaid conjurations, rehearsing them several times together, and he will come without doubt, if not at the first or second time of rehearsing. But if he do not come, add the "Spirits' Chain" unto the end of the aforesaid conjurations, and he will be forced to come, even if he be bound in chains, for the chains must break off from him, and he will be at liberty:

THE GENERAL CURSE, CALLED THE SPIRITS' CHAIN, AGAINST ALL SPIRITS THAT REBEL

O THOU wicked and disobedient spirit N., because thou hast rebelled, and hast not obeyed nor regarded my words which I have rehearsed; they being all glorious and incomprehensible names of the true GOD, the maker and creator of thee and of me, and of all the world; I DO by the power of these names the which no creature is able to resist, curse thee into the depth of the Bottomless Abyss, there to remain unto the Day of Doom in chains, and in fire and brimstone unquenchable, unless thou forthwith appear here before this Circle, in this triangle to do my will. And, therefore, come thou quickly and peaceably, in and by these names of GOD, ADONAI, ZABAOTH, ADONAI, AMIORAN; come thou! come thou! for it is the King of Kings, even ADONAI, who commandeth thee.

WHEN thou shalt have rehearsed thus far, but still be cometh not, then write thou his seal on parchment and put thou it into a strong black box; with brimstone, assafœtida, and such like things that bear a stinking smell; and then bind the box up round with an iron wire, and bang it upon the point of thy sword, and hold it over the fire of charcoal; and say as followeth unto the fire first, it being placed toward that quarter whence the Spirit is to come:

THE CONJURATION OF THE FIRE

I CONJURE thee, O fire, by him who made thee and all other creatures for good in the world, that thou torment, burn, and consume this Spirit N., for everlasting. I condemn thee, thou Spirit N., because thou art disobedient and obeyest not my commandment, nor keepest the precepts of the LORD THY GOD, neither wilt thou obey me nor mine invocations, having thereby called thee forth, 1, who am the servant of the MOST HIGH AND IMPERIAL LORD GOD OF HOSTS, IEHOVAH, I who am dignified and fortified by His celestial power and permission, and yet thou comest not to answer these my propositions here made unto thee. For the which thine averseness and contempt thou art guilty of great disobedience and rebellion, and therefore shall I excommunicate thee, and destroy thy name and seal, the which I have enclosed in this box; and shall burn thee in the immortal fire and bury thee in immortal oblivion; unless thou immediately come and appear visibly and affably, friendly and courteously here unto me before this Circle, in this triangle, in a form comely and fair, and in no wise terrible, hurtful, or frightful to me or any other creature whatsoever upon the face of earth. And thou shalt make rational answers unto my requests, and perform all my desires in all things, that I shall make unto thee.

AND if he come not even yet, thou shalt say as followeth:

THE GREATER CURSE

Now, O thou Spirit N., since thou art still pernicious and disobedient, and wilt not appear unto me to answer unto such things as I would have desired of thee, or would have been satisfied in; I do in the name, and by the power and dignity of the Omnipresent and Immortal Lord God of Hosts IEHOVAH TETRAGRAMMATON, the only creator of Heaven, and Earth, and Hell, and all that is therein, who is the marvellous Disposer of all things both visible and invisible, curse thee, and deprive thee of all thine office, joy, and place; and I do bind thee in the depths of the Bottomless Abyss there to remain until the Day of Judgment, I say into the Lake of Fire and Brimstone which is prepared for all rebellious, disobedient, obstinate, and pernicious spirits. Let all the company of Heaven curse thee! Let the sun, moon, and all the stars curse thee! Let the LIGHT and all the hosts of Heaven curse thee into the fire unquenchable, and into the torments unspeakable. And as thy name and seal contained in this box chained and bound up, shall be choken in sulphurous stinking substances, and burned in this material fire; so in the name IEHOVAH and by the power and dignity of these three names, TETRAGRAMMATON, ANAPHAXETON, and PRIMEUMATON, I do cast thee, O thou wicked and disobedient Spirit N., into the Lake of Fire which is prepared for the damnéd and accurséd spirits, and there to remain unto the day of doom, and never more to be remembered before the face of GOD, who shall come to judge the quick, and the dead, and the world, by fire.

THEN the exorcist must put the box into the fire, and by-and-by the Spirit will come, but as soon as he is come, quench the fire that the box is in, and make a sweet perfume, and give him welcome and a kind entertainment, showing unto him the Pentacle that is at tile bottom of your vesture covered with a linen cloth, saying:

THE ADDRESS UNTO THE SPIRIT UPON HIS COMING

BEHOLD thy confusion if thou refusest to be obedient! Behold the Pentacle of Solomon which I have brought here before thy presence! Behold the person of the exorcist in the midst of the exorcism; him who is arméd by GOD and without fear; him who potently invocateth thee and calleth thee forth unto appearance; even him, thy master, who is called OCTINIMOS. Wherefore make rational answer unto my demands, and prepare to be obedient unto thy master in the name of the Lord:

BATHAL OR VATHAT
RUSHING UPON
ABRAC!
ABEOR COMING UPON
ABERER

THEN he or they will be obedient, and bid thee ask what thou wilt, for he or they be subjected by God to fulfil our desires and commands. And when he or they shall have appeared and showed himself or themselves humble and meek, then shalt thou rehearse:

THE WELCOME UNTO THE SPIRIT

WELCOME Spirit N., O most noble king (or kings)! I say thou art welcome unto me, because I have called thee through Him who has created Heaven, and Earth, and Hell, and all that is in them contained, and because also thou hast obeyed. By that same power by the which I have called thee forth, I bind thee, that thou remain affably and visibly here before this Circle (or before this Circle and in this triangle) so constant and so long as I shall have occasion for thy presence; and not to depart without my license until thou hast duly and faithfully performed my will without any falsity.

THEN standing in the midst of the Circle, thou shall stretch forth thine hand in a gesture of command and say:

"BY TIME PENTACLE OF SOLOMON HAVE I CALLED THEE! GIVE UNTO ME A TRUE ANSWER."

Then let the exorcist state his desires and requests.

And when the evocation is finished thou shalt license the Spirit to depart thus:

THE LICENSE TO DEPART

O THOU Spirit N., because thou hast-diligently answered unto my, demands, and hast been very ready and willing to come at my call, I do here license thee to depart unto thy proper place; without causing harm or danger unto man or beast. Depart, then, I say, and be thou very ready to come at my call, being duly exorcised and conjured by the sacred rites of magic. I charge thee to withdraw peaceably and quietly, and the peace of GOD be ever continued between thee and me I AMEN!

AFTER thou hast given the Spirit license to depart, thou art not to go out of the circle until he or they be gone, and until thou shalt have made prayers and rendered thanks unto God for the great blessings He hath bestowed upon thee in granting thy desires, and delivering thee from all the malice of the enemy the devil.

Also note! Thou mayest command these spirits into the Vessel of Brass in the same manner as thou dost into the triangle, by saying: "that thou dost forthwith appear before this Circle, in this Vessel of Brass, in a fair and comely shape," etc., as hath been shown in the foregoing conjurations.

EXPLANATION OF CERTAIN NAMES USED IN THIS BOOK LEMEGETON

Eheie. Kether. Almighty God, whose dwelling is in the highest Heavens:

Haioth. The great King of Heaven, and of all the powers therein:

Methratton. And of all the holy hosts of Angels and Archangels:

Reschith. Hear the prayers of Thy servant who putteth his trust in Thee:

Hagalgalim. Let thy Holy Angels be commanded to assist me at this time and at all times.

Iehovah. God Almighty, God Omnipotent, hear my prayer:

Hadonat. Command Thy Holy Angels above the fixed stars:

Ophanim. To be assisting and aiding Thy servant:

Iophiel. That I may command all spirits of air, water, fire, earth, and hell:

Masloth. So that it may tend unto Thy glory and unto the good of man.

Iehovah. God Almighty, God Omnipotent, hear my prayer:

Elohim. God with us, God be always present with us.

Binah. Strengthen us and support us, both now and for ever:

Aralim. In these our undertakings, which we perform but as instruments in Thy hands:

Zabbathi. In the hands of Thee, the great God of Sabäoth.

Hesel. Thou great God, governor and creator of the planets, and of the Host of Heaven:

Hasmalim Command them by Thine almighty power:

Zelez. To be now present and assisting to us Thy poor servants, both now and for ever.

Elohim Geber. Most Almighty and eternal and ever living Lord God:

Seraphim. Command Thy seraphim:

Camael, Madim.   To attend on us now at this time, to assist us, and to defend us from all perils and dangers.

Eloha. O Almighty God! be present with us both now and for ever:

Tetragrammaton. And let thine Almighty power and presence ever guard and protect us now and for ever:

Raphael. Let thy holy angel Raphael wait upon us at this present and for ever:

Schemes or **Shemesh**. To assist us in these our undertakings.

Iehovah. God Almighty, God Omnipotent, hear my prayer:

Sabäoth. Thou great God of Sabäoth:

Netzah or **Netzach**. All-seeing God:

Elohim. God be present with us, and let thy presence be now and always present with us:

Haniel. Let thy holy angel Haniel come and minister unto us at this present.

Sabäoth. O thou great God of Sabäoth, be present with us at this time and for ever:

Hodben. Let Thine Almighty power defend us and protect us, both now and for ever:

Michael. Let Michael, who is, under Thee, general of thy heavenly host:

Cochab. Come and expel all evil and danger from us both now and for ever.

Sadai. Thou great God of all wisdom and knowledge:

Jesal. Instruct Thy poor and most humble servant:

Cherubim. By Thy holy cherubim:

Gabriel. By Thy Holy Angel Gabriel, who is the Author and Messenger of good tidings:

Levanah. Direct and support us at this present and for ever.

THE EXPLANATION OF THE TWO TRIANGLES IN THE PARCHMENT

Alpha And Omega. Thou, O great God, Who art the beginning and the end:

Tetragrammaton. Thou God of Almighty power, be ever present with us to guard and protect us, and let Thy Holy Spirit and presence be now and always with us:

Soluzen. I command thee, thou Spirit of whatsoever region thou art, to come unto this circle:

Halliza. And appear in human shape:

Bellator or **Ballaton**. And speak unto us audibly in our mother-tongue:

Bellonoy or **Bellony**. And show, and discover unto us all treasure that thou knowest of, or that is in thy keeping, and deliver it unto us quietly:

Hallii. Hra. And answer all such questions as we may demand without any defect now at this time.

AN EXPLANATION OF SOLOMON'S TRIANGLE

Anephezeton. Thou great God of all the Heavenly Host:

Primeumaton. Thou Who art the First and Last, let all spirits be subject unto us, and let the Spirit be bound in this triangle, which disturbs this place:

Michael. By Thy Holy Angel Michael, until I shall discharge him.

HERE ENDETH
THIS FIRST BOOK OF THE LEMEGETON,
WHICH IS CALLED THE GOETIA.

Yse Conjuratiouns of ye Books Goetia in ye Lemegeton which Solomoun ye Kynge did give unto Lemuel hys sonne rendered into ye Magicall or Angelike Language by our Illustrious and ever Glorious Frater, ye Wise Perdurabo, that Myghtye Chiefe of ye Rosy-Cross Fraternitye, now sepulchred in ye Vault of ye Collegium S.S. And soe may we doe alle!

ATTE YE BATHES OF ART.

Asperges me, Domine, hyssopo, et mundabor:
Lavabis me, et super nivem dealbabor

ATTE YE INDUYNGE OF YE HOLY VESTURES.

In the mystery of these vestures of the Holy Ones, I gird up my power in the girdles of righteousness and truth in the power of the Most High: Ancor: Amacor: Amides: Theodonias: Anitor: let be mighty my power: let it endure for ever: in the power of Adonai, to whom the praise and the glory shall be; whose end cannot be.

YE FYRSTE CONJOURATIOUN.

I invoke and move thee, O thou, Spirit N.: and being exalted above ye in the power of the Most High, I say unto thee, Obey! in the name Beralensis, Baldachiensis, Paumachia, and Apologiae Sedes: and of the mighty ones who govern, spirits, Liachidae and ministers of the House of Death: and by the Chief Prince of the seat of Apologia in the Ninth Legion, I do invoke. thee and by invoking conjure thee. And being exalted above ye in the power of the, Most High., I say unto thee, Obey! in the name of him who spake and it was, to whom all creatures and things obey. Moreover I, whom God made in the likeness of God, who is the. creator according to his living breath, stir thee up in the name which is the voice of wonder of the mighty God, El, strong and unspeakable, O thou Spirit N. And I say to thee obey, in the name of him who spake and it was; and in every one of ye, O ye names of God! Moreover in the names Adonai, El., Elohim., Elohi, Ehyeh Asher Ehyeh, Zabaoth, Elion, Iah, Tetragrammaton, Shaddai, Lord

God Most High, I stir thee up; and in our strength I say Obey! O Spirit N. Appear unto His servants in a moment; before the circle in the likeness of a man; and visit me in peace. And in the ineffable name Tetragrammaton Iehovah, I say, Obey! whose mighty sound being exalted in power the pillars are divided, the winds of the firmament groan aloud; the fire burns not; the earth moves in earthquakes; and all things of the house of heaven and earth and the dwelling-place of darkness are as earthquakes, and are in torment, and are confounded in thunder. Come forth, O Spirit N. in. a moment: let thy dwelling-place be empty, apply unto us the secrets of Truth and obey my power. Come forth, visit us in peace, appear unto my eyes; be friendly: Obey the living breath! For I stir thee up in the name of the God of Truth who liveth for ever, Helioren. Obey the living breath, therefore continually unto the end as my thoughts appear to my eyes: therefore be friendly: speaking the secrets of Truth in voice and in understanding.

YE SECOUNDE CONJOURATIOUN

I invoke thee, and move thee, and stir thee up O Spirit N. appear unto my eyes before the circle in the likeness of a man in the names and by the name Iah and Vau, which Adam spake and in the name of God, Agla, which Lot spake: and it was as pleasant deliverers unto him and his house and in the name Ioth which Iacob spake in the voice of the Holy ones who cast him down, and it was also as pleasant deliverers in the anger of his brother and in the name Anaphaxeton, which Aaron spake and it was as the Secret Wisdom and in the name Zabaoth which Mosheh spake, and all things of water were as blood; and in the name Asher Ehyeh Oriston, which Mosheh spake, and all waters were bringing forth creatures who wax strong, which lifted up unto the houses, which destroy all things and in the name of Elion which Mosheh spake, and it was as stones from the firmament of wrath, such as was not in the ages of Time the beginning of the Earth and in the name of Adni, which Mosheh spake and there appeared creatures of earth who destroyed what the big stones did not: and in the name Schema Amathia, which Ioshua invoked, and the Sun remained over ye, O ye hills the seats of Gibeon, and in the names

Alpha and Omega which Daniel spake, and destroyed Bel and the Dragon: and in the name Emmanuel which the sons of God sang praises in the midst of the burning plain, and flourished in conquest: and in the name Hagios, and by the Throne of Adni, and in Ischyros, Athanatos, Paracletos: and in O Theos, Ictros, Athanatos. And in these names of secret truth, Agla, On, Tetragrammaton, do I invoke and move thee. And in these names, and all things that are the names of the God of Secret Truth who liveth for ever, the All-Powerful. I invoke and stir thee up, O spirit N. Even by him who spake it was, to whom all creatures are obedient and in the Extreme Justice and Anger of God; and by the veil(?) that is before the glory of God, mighty; and by the creatures of living breath before the Throne whose eyes are east and west; by the fire in the fire of just Glory of the Throne; by the Holy ones of Heaven; and by the secret wisdom of God, I, exalted in power, stir thee up. Appear before this circle; obey in all things that I say; in the seal Basdathea Baldachia; and in this Name Primeumaton, which Mosheh spake, and the earth was divided, and Korah, Dathan, and Abiram fell in the depth. Therefore obey in all things, O spirit N., obey thy creation. Come thou forth: appear unto my eyes; visit us in peace, be friendly; come forth in the 24th of a moment; obey my power, speaking the secrets of Truth in voice and in understanding!

YE CONSTRAYNTE.

I stir thee up, O spirit N. in all things that are the names of glory and power of God the Great One who is greater than understanding, Adni Ihvh Tzabaoth, come forth in the 24th of a moment, let Thy dwelling-place be empty; apply thyself unto the secret truth and obey my power: appear unto my eyes, visit us in peace, speaking the secrets of truth in voice and understanding. I stir thee up and move thee, O spirit N., in all the names that I have said, and I add these one and six names wherein Solomon, the lord of the secret wisdom, placed yourselves, spirits of wrath, in a vessel, Adonai,. Preyai Tetragrammaton, Anaphaxeton Inessenfatoal, Pathtomon and Itemon: appear before this circle; obey in all things my power. And as thou art he that obeys not and comes not I shall be in thy power, O God Most High that liveth for ever, who is the creator of all things in six days Eie,

Saraye, and in my power in the name Prieumaton that ruleth over the palaces of heaven, Curse Thee, and destroy thy seat, joy, and power; and I bind thee in the depth of Abaddon, to remain until the day of judgment whose end cannot be. And I bind thee in the fire of sulphur mingled with poison and the seas of fire and sulphur: come, forth, therefore, obey my power and appear before, this circle. Therefore come forth in the name of the Holy Ones Zabaoth, Adonai, Amioran. Come! for I am Adonai who stir thee up.

YE POTENT INVOCATIOUN OF HYS KYNGE.

O thou great powerful governor Amaimon, who reigneth exalted in the power of the only El above all spirits in the kingdoms of the East, (South, West, North), I invoke and move thee in the name of the true God, and in God whom thou worshippest: and in the, seal of thy creation: and in the mighty names of God, Iehevohe Tetragrammaton, who cast thee down from Heaven, thou and the spirits of darkness, and in all the names of the mighty God who is the creator of Heaven and earth, and the dwelling of darkness, and all things and in their power and brightness; and in the name Primeumaton who reigns over the palaces of Heaven. Bring forth, I say, the spirit N.; bring him forth in the 24th of a moment let his dwelling be, empty until he visits us in peace, speaking the secrets of truth; until he obey my power and his creation in the power of God, El, who is the Creator and doth dispose of all things, heaven, firmament, earth, and the dwelling of darkness.

YE GENERALL CURSE.

YCLEPT YE SPIRITS' CHAYNE, AGAINST ALL SPIRITS YT REBELLE.

O thou wicket spirit N. that obeyeth not, because I made a law and invoked the names of the glorious and ineffable God of Truth, the creator of all, and thou obeyest not the mighty sounds that I make: therefore I curse thee in the depth of Abaddon to remain until the day of judgment in torment in fire and in sulphur without end, until thou appear before our will and obey my power. Come, therefore, in the 24th of a moment, before the circle in the triangle in this name and by this name of God, Adni, Tzabaoth, Adonai, Amioran. Come! Come! for it is the Lord of Lords Adni, that stirreth thee up.

YE CONJOURATIOUN OF YE FYRE.

I stir thee up, O thou fire, in him who is thy Creator and of all creatures. Torment, burn, destroy the spirit N. always whose end cannot be, I judge thee in judgment and in extreme justice, O spirit N., because thou art he that obeyeth not my power and obeyeth not that law which the Lord God made, and obeyeth not the Mighty Sounds and the Living Breath which I invoke, which I send: Come forth, I, who am the Servant of the game Most High governor Lord God powerful, Iehovohe, I who am exalted in power and am mighty in his power above ye, O thou who comest not giving obedience and faith to him that liveth and triumpheth. Therefore I say the judgment: I curse thee and destroy the name N. and the seal N., which I have placed in this dwelling of poison, and I burn thee in fire whose end cannot be; and I cast thee down unto the seas of torment, out of which thou shalt not rise until thou come to my eyes: visit me in peace: be friendly before the circle in the △ in the 24th of a moment in the likeness of a man not unto the terror of the sons of men the creatures or all things on the face of the earth. Obey my power like reasoning creatures; obey the living breath, the law which I speak.

YE GRETER CURSE.

Hearken to me, O ye Heavens! O thou Spirit N. because thou art the disobedient one who is wicked and appearest not, speaking the secrets of truth according to the, living breath; I, exalted in the power of God, the All powerful, the center of the circle, powerful God who liveth, whose end cannot be., Iehevohe Tetragrammaton,, the only creator of heaven, earth, and dwelling of darkness and, all that is in their palaces; who disposeth in secret wisdom of all things in darkness and light: Curse thee and cast thee down and destroy thy seat, joy and power, and I bind thee in the depths of Abaddon, to remain until the day of judgment whose end cannot be, I say, unto the seas of fire and sulphur which I have prepared for the wicked spirits that obey not; the sons of iniquity.

Let the company of heaven curse thee!

Let the sun, moon, all the stars curse thee!

Let the light and all the Holy Ones of Heaven curse thee unto the burning flame that liveth for ever, and unto the torment unspeakable!

And even as thy name and seal, which I have put in this dwelling of poison, shall be in torment among creatures of sulphur and bitter sting, burning in fire of earth, in them Iehevohe and exalted in power in these three names, Tetragrammaton Anaphaxeton, Primeumaton, I cast thee down, O wicked spirit N. unto the seas of fire and sulphur which are prepared for the wicked spirits that obey not, the sons of iniquity, to remain until the day of judgment; let the Mercies of God forget thee; let the face of God forget the face of N. who will not see light: let God forget, I say that shall be the balance of justice over the sons of living breath and death and the world, by fire.

YE ADDRESSE UNTO YE SPIRIT ON HYS COMING.

Behold! I confound thee as thou art he that obeys not! Behold the mysteries of the seal of Solomon which I bring forth unto thy power and presence! Behold the creator, the centre of the circle of the living breath; he that is exalted in the power of God and shall not see unto the terror: he that powerfully invoketh and stirreth thee up unto visible appearance: he, the lord of thy governments whose Name is called Octinomos.

Obey, therefore, my power as a reasoning creature -in the name of the Lord.

YE WELCOME UNTO YE SPIRIT DYGNYTIE.

I am he that is looking with gladness upon thee, O thou spirit . . .
N. beautiful and praiseworthy! with gladness I say, because thou
art called in him who is creator of Heaven and earth and the
dwelling of darkness, and all things that are in their palaces, and
because thou art the servant of obedience. In these the power by
which thou art obedient to the living breath, I bind thee to remain
visible to our eyes in power and presence as the servant of fealty
before the circle until I say "Descend unto thy dwelling" until the
living breath of the voice of the Lord is according to the law which
shall be given unto thee.

By the seal of the secret wisdom of Solomon thou art called!

Obey the mighty sounds! obey the living breath of the voice of the
Lord!

Follows ye charge.

YE LICENSE TO YE SPIRIT YT HE MAYE DEPART.

O thou Spirit N. because thou art the servant of fealty and
obedience, and because thou art he that obeyeth my power and
thy creation; therefore I say Descend unto thy dwelling, obey the
law which I have made, without terror to the sons of men,
creatures, all things upon the surface of the earth.

Descend therefore I say, and be thou as stewards of Time; come
forth in a moment, even as servants that hearken to the voice of
the Lord; in the moment in which I invoke thee and stir thee up
and move thee in the, mysteries of the secret wisdom of the
Creator!

Descend unto thy dwelling place in pleasure: let there be the
mercies of God upon thee: be friendly in continuing; whose long
continuance shall be comforters unto all creatures. Amen.

THE ART THEURGIA GOETIA

In this following treatise you have the names of the Chief Spirits with several of the Ministring Spirits that are under them, with their Seals or charactors which are to be worn as a Lamen on your breast, for without that the Spirit that has appeared will not obey to do your will.

The office of these Spirits is all one, for what one can do the others can do the same, they can show & discover all things that are hidden, and done in the world & can fetch & carry & do any thing that is to be done or contained in any of the 4 Elements, Fire, Air, Earth or Water, & also the secrets of Kings or any other persons or person, let it be in what kind it will.

These are by nature good & evil, that is the one part is good & the other part is Evil, they are governed by their Princes, & each Prince hath his abode in the points of the Compass, as is showed in the following figure, therefore when you have a desire to call any of the Princes or any of their servants, you are to direct your self towards that point of the Compass the King or Prince has his mansion or place of Abode, & you cannot well err in your operations, note every Prince is to have his Conjuration, yet all of one form, excepting the name and place of the Spirit for in that they must change & differ, also the seals of the Spirits are to be changed accordingly.
As for the garments & other materials, they are spoken of in the Book Goetia, aforesaid.

The Forme of the figure which Discovers the orders of the 31 Kings or Princes with their Servants & Ministers, for when the King is found his subjects are easy to be found out.

The Figure Followeth:

South
Caspiel

S &by E · S &by W
SSE · SSW
SE &by S · SW &by S
SE · SW
SE &by E · SW &by W
ESE · WSW
E &by S · W &by S
East · West
E &by N · W &by N
ENE · WNW
NE &by E · NW &by W
NE · NW
NE &by N · NW &by N
NNE · NNW
N &by E · N &by W
North
Demoriel

Carnesiel — Amenadiel

Summer Hot · Air · Fire · Dry · Earth · Water · Cold · Moist

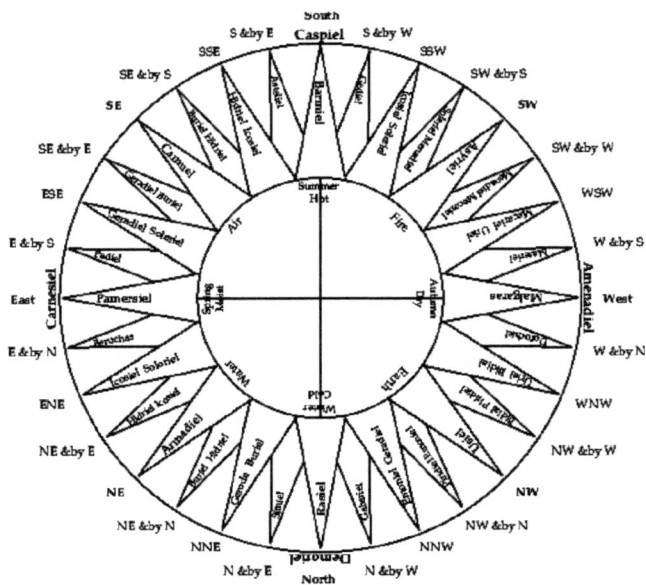

You may perceive by this figure that 20 of these Kings have then fixed mansions & continue in one place, & the others are movable & are sometimes in one place & sometimes another & sometimes in another more or less.

Therefore it is no matter which way you stand with your face when you desire to call them or their servants. Carnesiel is the most chief & great Emperor ruling the East, who hath 1000 great Dukes & 100 Lessor Dukes under him, besides 500,000,000,000 of ministring Spirits which are more inferior than the Dukes, whereof we shall make no mention but only 12 of the chief Dukes & their seals because they are sufficient for practise.

CARNESIEL

When you call Carnesiel either by day or by night, there Attend him 60,000,000,000,000 Dukes, but when you call any of his Dukes, there never Attends above 300 & sometimes not above 10.

THE SEALS OF HIS 12 DUKES:

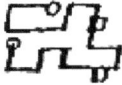

ORVICH SEAL

ARMANY SEAL

BENOHAM SEAL

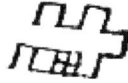

MYREZYN SEAL

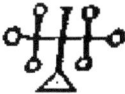

VADRIEL SEAL

BUCAFAS SEAL

BEDARY SEAL

CUMERZEL SEAL

ZABRIEL SEAL

CAPRIEL SEAL

ARIFEL SEAL

LAPHOR SEAL

The Conjuration:
"I conjure thee O thou great mighty & potent Prince Carnesiel,
&c."

146

CASPIEL

Caspiel is the Chiefest Emperor Ruling the South who hath 200 great Dukes & 400 lesser Dukes under him besides 1,000,200,000,000 of Ministring Spirits which are much inferior & whereof we [saith Solomon] shall make no mention but only of these 12 being the chief Dukes & their seals for they are sufficient for practise. Each of these 12 Dukes have 2660 under Dukes apeace to Attend them, whereof some of them come along with him when he is invoked but they are very stubborn & churlish.

THE SEALS OF HIS DUKES FOLLOW:

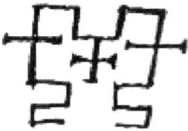

CHARIEL SEAL

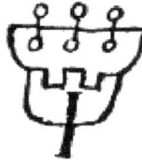

VUSIEL SEAL

TEMOL SEAL

MARAS SEAL

CAMORR SEAL

BUDARIJM SEAL

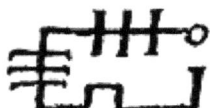

ARIAIEL SEAL

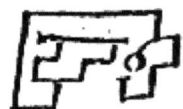

LARMOL SEAL

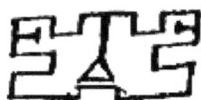

AMBRI SEAL

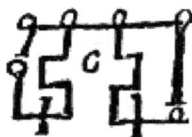

GERIEL SEAL

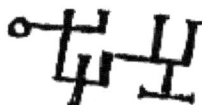

OTIEL SEAL

CAMOR SEAL

The Conjuration:
"I Conjure thee O thou Mighty & Potent Prince Caspiel, &c."

AMENADIEL

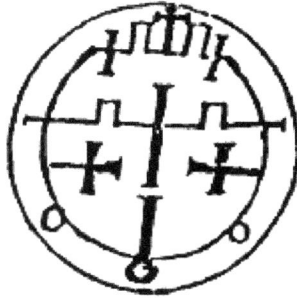

Amenadiel is the great Emperor of the West who hath 300 great Dukes & 500 lesser Dukes besides 40,000,030,000,100,000 other ministring Spirits more inferior to Attend him, whereof we shall not make any mention but only 12 of the Chief Dukes & their seals which is sufficient for practice.

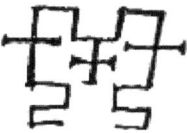

CHARIEL SEAL

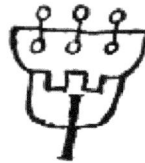

VUSIEL SEAL

TEMOL SEAL

MARAS SEAL

CAMORR SEAL

BUDARIJM SEAL

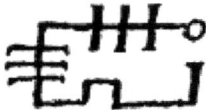

ARIAIEL SEAL

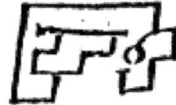

LARMOL SEAL

AMBRI SEAL

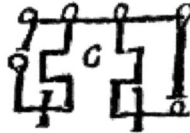

GERIEL SEAL

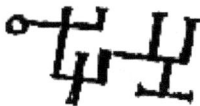

OTIEL SEAL

CAMOR SEAL

The Conjuration:
"I conjure thee O thou great & mighty & potent prince Amenadiel,
who is the Emperor & chief King ruling in the Dominion of the
West, &c "

DEMORIEL

Demoriel is the great & mighty Emperor of the North, who hath 400 Great Dukes & 600 lesser Dukes with 700,000,800,000,000,000 servants under his command to Attend him, whereof we shall make no mention but of 12 of the Chief Dukes & their seals which is sufficient for practise. Note: each of these Dukes hath 1140 servants who Attend them as need requireth, for when the Duke is called for, & you have more to do than ordinary, he hath more servants to Attend him.

THE SEALS OF THE 12 DUKES:

ARMBIEL SEAL

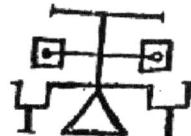

CHOMIEL SEAL

CABARIM SEAL

MONANDOR SEAL

BURISIEL SEAL

DIRIEL SEAL

CARNOL SEAL

MADOR SEAL

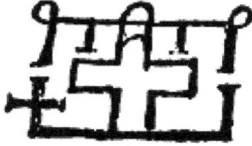

DUBILON SEAL

MODER SEAL

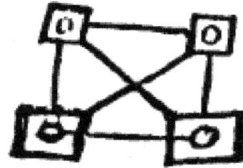

CHURIBAL SEAL

DABRINOS SEAL

The Conjuration:
"I Conjure thee O thou great & mighty & Potent Prince
Demoriel, &c."

PAMERSIEL

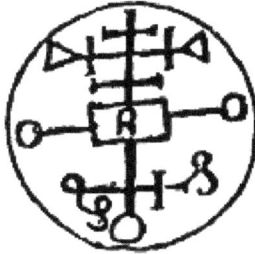

Pamersiel is the first & chief Spirit ruling in the East under Canesiel who hath a thousand Spirits under him, (none) is to be called in the daytime but with great care for they are very lofty & stubborn, whereof we shall make mention of 11.

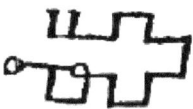

MADRIEL SEAL

EBRA SEAL

SOTHEANS SEAL

MADRES SEAL

ABRULGES SEAL

ORMENU SEAL

ITULES SEAL

RABLION SEAL

HAMORPHOL SEAL

ITRASBIEL SEAL

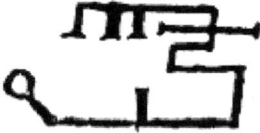

ANEYR SEAL

SOLOMON'S TABLE

The Conjuration:
"I conjure thee, O thou mighty & potent Prince Pamersiel who Ruleth as a King in the Dominion of the East, &c."

PADIEL

The 2nd. Spirit in order under the Empire of the East, is Padiel, he Ruleth in the East & By South as a King & Governeth 10,000 Spirits by day & 200,000 by night besides several thousand under them, they are all naturally good & may be trusted, Solomon saith those Spirits hath no power of themselves but what is given them by their Prince Padiel, therefore he hath made no mention of any of their names, because if any of them be called they cannot appear without the leave of Prince Padiel, as is declared before Pamersiel.

The Conjuration:
"I Conjure thee O thou mighty & Potent prince Padiel, who rules as chief prince in the Dominion or the East & By south, &c ".

CAMUEL

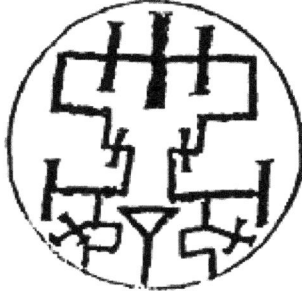

The third Spirit in Order (which) is under the Chief King of the East is Camuel, who ruleth as a King in the South East part of the World, who hath several Spirits under his command whereas we shall make mention of 10 that belong to the Day & as many that belong to the Night, & each of these have 10 servants to attend them, excepting Camyel, Citgaras, Calym, Meras, for they have 100 apiece to attend them, but Tediol, Moriol & Tugaros, they have none at all. They appear all in a very beautiful form & very courteously in the Night as well as the Day, and they are as followeth with their Seals.

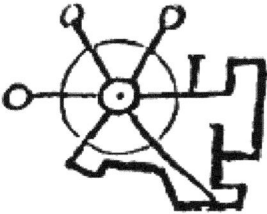

ORPENIEL SEAL

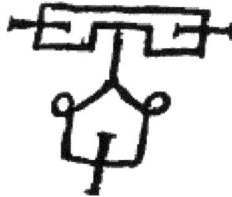

PARIELS SEAL

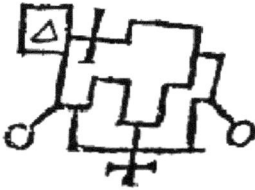

CHAMIJELS SEAL

CARIELS SEAL

BUDIEL SEAL

NERIELS SEAL

ELEARYS SEAL

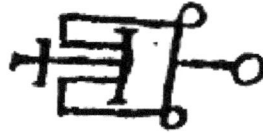

DANIELS SEAL

CITGARAS SEAL

OMIELS SEAL

CAMUEL

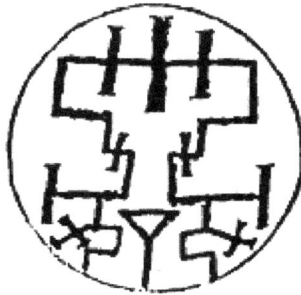

THE NAMES OF CAMUELS SERVANTS BELONGING TO THE
NIGHT & THEIR SEALS FOLLOW:

ASNIELS SEAL

MORAS SEAL

CALYMS SEAL

(?) SEAL

DOBIELS SEAL

TODIEL SEAL

NODARS SEAL

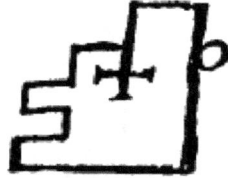

MORIEL(S) SEAL

PHANIELS SEAL

TUAROS SEAL

The Conjuration:
"I Conjure thee O thou mighty & Potent Prince, &c."

ASTELIEL

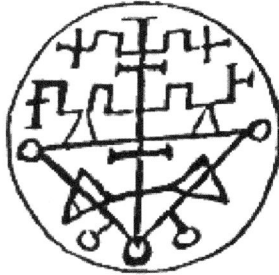

The 4th Spirit in order is Asteliel, he governeth as King under Carnesiel in the South & by East, be hath 10 chief Spirits belonging to the Day & 20 to the Night, under whom are 3 principal Spirits & under these as many, whereof we shall make mention of 8 of the chief presidents belonging to the Day & as many to the Night, every one hath 20 servants at his command, they are all very courteous & loving & beautiful to behold & they are as followeth with there their seals.

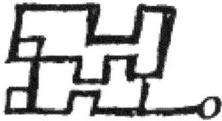

MARIOL HIS SEAL

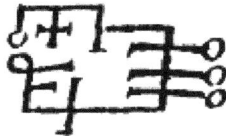

CHARAS SEAL

PARNIEL SEAL

ARATIEL SEAL

CUBIEL SEAL

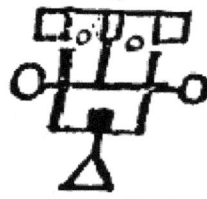

ANIEL SEAL

OTIEL SEAL

OTHIEL SEAL

ASTELIEL

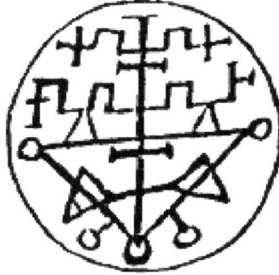

HERE FOLLOWETH THE 8 SERVANTS THAT BELONG TO THE
NIGHT:

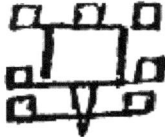

SARIEL SEAL

ASAHEL SEAL

AROAM SEAL

EURIEL SEAL

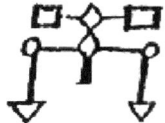

CHAMOS SEAL

ASPHIEL SEAL

BUFAR SEAL

MELAS SEAL

Those Spirits which belong to the Night (are) to be called in the Night, & those of the Day in the Day.

The Conjuration:
"I conjure thee O thou Mighty & Potent Prince Asteliel &c."

BARMIEL

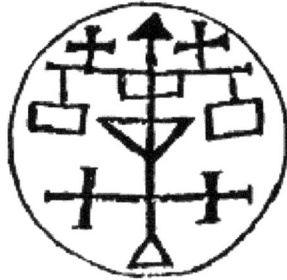

The 5th. Spirit in order is Barmiel, he is the first & chief Spirit under Caspiel, the Emperor of the South, he governs as King under Caspiel & hath 10 Dukes for the Day & 20 for the Night to attend him to do his will, the which are all very good & willing to obey the Exorcist, whereof we shall make mention but of 8 that belong to the day & as many for the night, with their seals for they are sufficient for practise.

THE 8 DUKES WHICH BELONG TO THE NIGHT & THEIR SEALS UNDER BARMIEL:

BERBIS SEAL

MORCAZA SEAL

ACEREBA SEAL

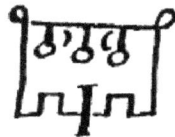

ASHIB SEAL

GABIR SEAL

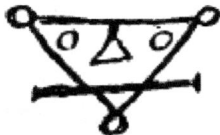

CARNET SEAL

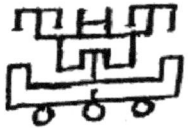

MARQUES SEAL

BAABAL SEAL

Those of the Day must be called in the Day, & those of the Night, in the Night.

The Conjuration:
"I conjure thee O thou mighty & Potent Prince Barmiel, &c."

GEDIEL

The 6th. Spirit in order, but the second under the Empire of the South is Gediel, who ruleth as King in the South & by West, who hath 20 chief Spirits to serve him in the Day & as many in the Night, & they have servants at their command whereof we shall make mention but of 8 of the chief Spirits that belong to the Day & as many that belong to the Night, who hath 20 servants apeice to attend them, when they are called forth to appearance, they are very loving and courteous, willing to do your will, you must call those in the Day that belong to the Day, & those in the Night that belong to the Night, whose names & seals are as followeth:

COTIEL SEAL

NARAS SEAL

SADIEL SEAL

AGRA SEAL

ASSABA SEAL

SABAS SEAL

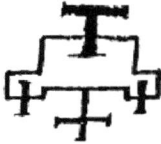

RECIEL SEAL

ANAEL SEAL

GEDIEL

HERE FOLLOWETH THE NAMES & SEALS OF THE 8 DUKES
THAT ARE UNDER GEDIEL & TO CALL BY NIGHT:

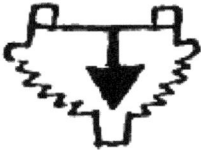

SARIEL SEAL

CIRECAS SEAL

ARAON SEAL

VRIEL SEAL

AGLAS SEAL

MISHEL SEAL

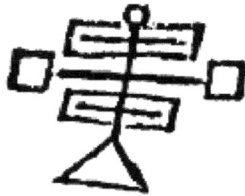

RANTIEL SEAL

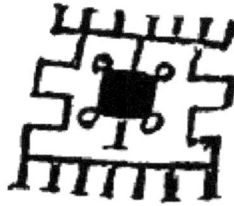

BARIEL SEAL

The Conjuration:
"I Conjure thee O thou Mighty & Potent Prince Gediel, &c."

ASYRIEL

Ruling in the Southwest part of the World, & hath 20 great Dukes to attend him in the Day & as many in the Night, who have under them several servants to attend them, & we mention 8 of the chief Dukes that belong to the Day & as many that belong to the Night, because they are sufficient for practise, & the first 4 that belong to the Day hath 40 servants apeice under them & so hath the first 4 that belong to the Night, & the last 4 of the Day, 20 & the last 4 of the Night 10 apeice. They are all good natured & willing to obey thee, those that are of the Day to be called in the Day, & those of the Night, in the Night, & these be their names & seals that followeth:

HIS 8 DUKES FOLLOW THAT BELONG TO THE DAY:

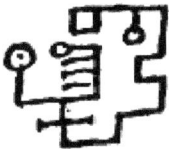

OLITORS SEAL

CARGA SEAL

RABAS SEAL

BUNIELS SEAL

ARISAT SEAL

ARIEL SEAL

CUOPIEL SEAL

MALUGEL SEAL

ASYRIEL

THE 8 DUKES THAT BELONG TO THE NIGHT:

AMIEL SEAL

CUSREL SEAL

MAROTT SEAL

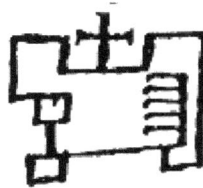

ONUEL SEAL

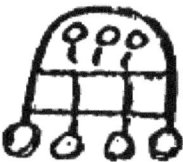

BUTER SEAL

ASPIEL SEAL

FIASCUA SEAL

HAMAS SEAL

The Conjuration:
"I Conjure thee O thou Mighty & Potent Prince Asyriel, who
rulest as a King, &c."

MASERIEL

The 8th. Spirit in order but the 4th. under the Empire of the South is called Maseriel, who ruleth as King in the Dominion of the West & by South, & hath a great number of Princes & Servants under him to Attend him, whereof we shall make mention of 12 of the chief spirits that attend him in the day time & 12 that attend & do his will in the night time, which is sufficient for practise, they are all good natured & willing to do your will in all things, those that are for the day are to be called in the day, & those for the night, in the night, their names & seals followeth & each Spirit hath 30 servants to attend him.

THE 12 SPIRITS THAT BELONG TO THE DAY FOLLOW:

MAYHUE HIS SEAL

CHARES SEAL

ZERIEL SEAL

ALIEL SEAL

AZIMEL SEAL

EARVIOL SEAL

ASSUEL SEAL

VESCUR SEAL

ROVIEL SEAL

PATIEL SEAL

ATMOT SEAL

ESPOEL SEAL

MASERIEL

THE SPIRITS BELONGING TO THE NIGHT.

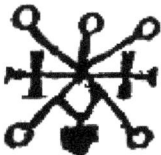

ARACH SEAL

ELIOL SEAL

SARMIEL SEAL

ATRIEL SEAL

BARAS SEAL

NOGOIOL SEAL

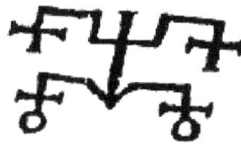

BADIEL SEAL

177

RABIEL SEAL

NARAS SEAL

AMOYR SEAL

ERAS SEAL

SDVAR SEAL

The Conjuration:
"I Conjure thee O thou Mighty & Potent Prince Maseriel, who
Ruleth as King, &c."

MALGARAS

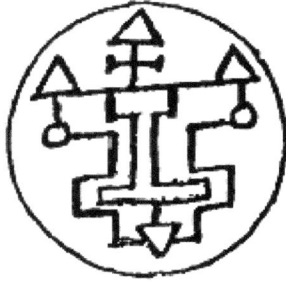

The 9th. Spirit in order but the first under the Empire of the West is called Malgaras, he ruleth in the Dominion of the West & hath 30 Dukes under him in the day & as many for the night, & they every one of them have 30 servants to attend them excepting Miliel, Barfas, Asper & Deiles for they have but 20 apeace. Arois & Basiel hath but 10, and they are all very courteous & will appear willing to do your will, they appear 2 & 2 at a time with their servants, those that are for the day to be called in the day, & those of the night in the night, their names &c. as followeth:

THE 12 DUKES THAT BELONG TO THE DAY FOLLOW:

CARIMIEL SEAL

RABIEL SEAL

AGOR SEAL

UDIEL SEAL

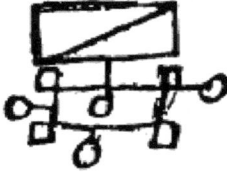

MELIEL SEAL

CASIEL HIS SEAL

ORIEL SEAL

ALISIEL SEAL

BORAS SEAL

CABIEL SEAL

BARFAS SEAL

AROIS SEAL

MALGARAS

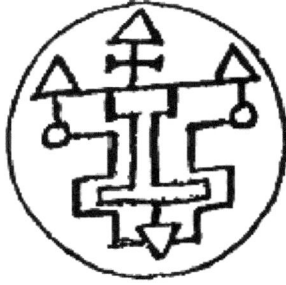

THE 12 DUKES BELONGING TO THE NIGHT FOLLOWETH:

ARAC SEAL

DEILAS SEAL

CUBI SEAL

RABAE SEAL

ASPIEL SEAL

ZAMOR SEAL

ASPER SEAL

BASIEL SEAL

LIBIEL SEAL

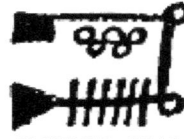

DODIEL SEAL

CARON SEAL

AMIEL SEAL

The Conjuration:
"I Conjure thee O thou mighty & potent Prince Malgaras, &c."

182

DAROCHIEL

The 10th. Spirit in order but the second under the Empire of the West is Dorochiel, who is a mighty Prince ruling in the West & by North & hath 40 Dukes to attend on him in the day & as many for the night, with an inumerable company of servants, whereof we shall make mention of 24 chief Dukes that belong to the day & as many for the night, with their seals as followeth. Note the 12 first that belong to the Day & of the Night hath 40 servants apiece to attend them when they appear, & all these of the day are to be called in the day, & those of the night in the night. Observe the planetary motions in calling, for the two first that belongeth to the day are intended for the first planetary hour, of the 2 next for second planetary hour of the day, & so successively on till you have gone through the day to the night, & through the night till you come to the 2 first of the day again, & they are all of good nature & are willing to obey & do your will, their names & seals are as followeth.

THE 24 DUKES THAT BELONG TO THE DAY, 12 BEFORE NOON & 12 AFTERNOON:

MAGAEL SEAL

ASPHOR SEAL

CARCIEL SEAL

DANAEL SEAL

GUDIEL SEAL

ARLINO SEAL

ABRIEL SEAL

CORUA SEAL

CHORIEL SEAL

EMUEL SEAL

TUBIEL SEAL

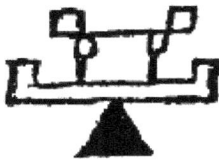

ETIEL SEAL

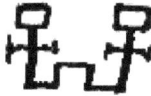

MORACH SEAL

SOVIAL SEAL

EASGEL SEAL

MAMEL SEAL

ALSHOR SEAL

LOMOR SEAL

CAVRON SEAL

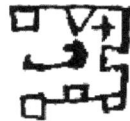

BUCIEL SEAL

SURIEL SEAL

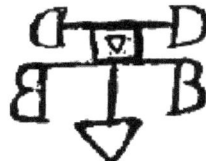

OMIEL SEAL

DIVIEL SEAL

LORGAT SEAL

185

HERE FOLLOWETH THE 24 DUKES THAT BELONG TO THE NIGHT. 12 OF THEM BEFORE MIDNIGHT & 12 AFTER:

NALIEL SEAL

GAYRES SEAL

SORIEL SEAL

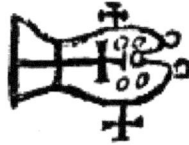

PELUSAR SEAL

PATIEL SEAL

BUDIS SEAL

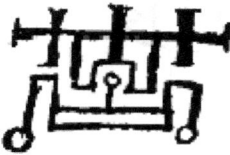

VRENIEL SEAL

PANIEL SEAL

OFISEL SEAL

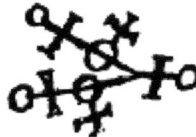

NARSIEL SEAL

DARBORI SEAL

ABAEL SEAL

186

MOMEL SEAL

AROZIOL SEAL

CURFAS SEAL

CHADRIEL SEAL

MOSIEL SEAL

GARIEL SEAL

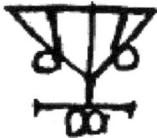

MEROTH SEAL

MAZIEL SEAL

PASIEL SEAL

CUSIJND SEAL

LIEL SEAL

LOBIEL SEAL

The Conjuration: "I Conjure thee, O thou mighty & Potent Prince
Dorochiel, &c."

USIEL

The 11th. Spirit in order but the third under the Emperor Amenadiel, is called Usiel, who is a mighty Prince ruling as King in the Northwest, he hath 40 diurnal & 40 nocturnal Dukes to attend him, in the day & in the night, whereof we shall make mention of 14 that belong to the day & as many for the night, which is sufficient for practise, the first 8 that belong to the day hath 40 servants apiece & the others 630 apiece, & the first 8 that belong to the night hath 40 servants apiece to attend them & the next 4 Dukes have 20 servants, and the last 2 Dukes hath 10 apiece, & they are very obedient & do willingly appear when they are called, they have more power to hide or discover treasure than any other Spirits saith Solomon, that is contained in this book Theurgia Goetia, & when you hide & would not have any thing taken away that is yours, make these 4 seals in virgin parchment & lay them with the treasure or where the treasure lyeth & it will never be found nor taken away, the names & seals of the Spirits are as followeth:

ALIMORIS SEAL

SEAFAR SEAL

AMETA SEAL

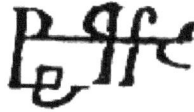

MAPUI SEAL

AMEN SEAL

AMANDIEL SEAL

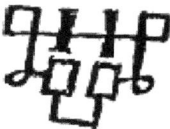

HERNE SEAL

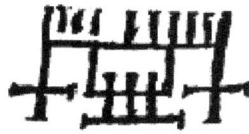

BARFU SEAL

SADFAR SEAL

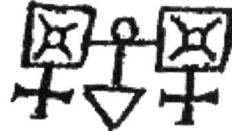

GARNAFU SEAL

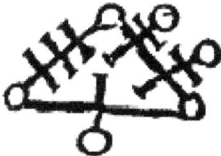

POTIEL SEAL

HISIAM SEAL

FABARIEL SEAL

VSIMEL SEAL

The Conjuration:
"I Conjure thee O thou mighty & Potent Prince Usiel, &c."

HERE FOLLOWETH THE 14 DUKES THAT BELONG TO THE NIGHT:

ANFEL SEAL

ASUREL SEAL

GODIEL SEAL

ALMOD SEAL

BARFOS SEAL

PATHIR SEAL

BURFA SEAL

NARAD SEAL

SADDIEL SEAL

LASPHORON SEAL

OFSIDIEL SEAL

ETHIEL SEAL

ADAN SEAL

SADDIEL SEAL

THE SEAL OF CABARIEL

The 12th. Spirit in order but the 4th. under the Empire of the West is Cabariel, who is a mighty prince ruling in the West & by North, he hath 50 Dukes to attend him in the day & as many for the night; with them are many servants to attend them, whereof we shall make mention but of 10 of the Chief Dukes that belong to the Day & as many for the Night, & every one of them hath 50 servants to give attendance when their master is called, & note that those that belong to the day are very good & willing to obey their master, & are to be called in the day time, & those of the night are by nature evil & disobediant & will deceive you if they can, & they are to be called in the night, their names & seals of them all are as followeth:

HIS 10 DUKES THAT BELONG TO THE DAY FOLLOWETH:

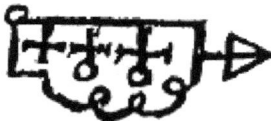

SATIFIEL SEAL

PENIEL SEAL

TARES SEAL

THALBOR SEAL

ETIMIEL SEAL

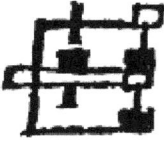

LADIEL SEAL

ELITEL SEAL

PARIUS SEAL

CUPHER SEAL

GODIEL SEAL

THE SEAL OF CABARIEL

THOSE OF THE NIGHT FOLLOWETH:

AFORIEL SEAL

ORIJM SEAL

ELIJSAM SEAL

MORIAS HIS SEAL

ANIEL SEAL

CAZSUL HIS SEAL

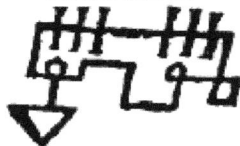

MADOR SEAL

DUBIEL HIS SEAL

UGIEL SEAL

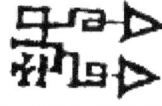

PANDOR HIS SEAL

The Conjuration:
"I Conjure thee O Thou mighty & Potent Prince &c,"

RAYSIEL HIS SEAL

The 13th. Spirit in order, is called Rasiel, he ruleth as King in the North; and hath 50 Dukes for the day, & as many for ye Night to attend him; and they have many servants under them Againe; for as to do their will &c. Whereof we shall make mention of 16 Chiefe Dukes that belong to the day because they are by nature good & willing to obey; & but 14 that belong to the Night because they are by nature evil & stuborne & disobedient & will not obey willingly. All these dukes that belong to the day hath 50 servants Apiece excepting the 6 last for they have but 30 apiece; & the 8 first that belong to the Night hath 40 servants Apiece; excepting the 4 next following for they have but 20 apiece; and the last but 10 apiece; Their Names and Seals are as followeth:

THE 16 THAT BELONG TO THE DAY:

BACIAR HIS SEAL

DUBARUS HIS SEAL

THOAC HIS SEAL

ARMENA HIS SEAL

SEQUIEL HIS SEAL

ALHADUR HIS SEAL

SADAR HIS SEAL

CHANAEL HIS SEAL

TERAGH HIS SEAL

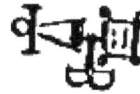

FURSIEL HIS SEAL

ASTIELL HIS SEAL

BETASIEL HIS SEAL

RAMICA HIS SEAL

MELCHA HIS SEAL

THARAS HIS SEAL

VBIEL HIS SEAL

THE 14 THAT BELONG TO THE NIGHT &C:

THARIEL HIS SEAL

QUIBDA HIS SEAL

PARAS HIS SEAL

BELSAY HIS SEAL

ARAYL HIS SEAL

MORAEL HIS SEAL

CULMAR HIS SEAL

SARACH HIS SEAL

LAZABA HIS SEAL

AREPACH HIS SEAL

ALEASY HIS SEAL

LAMAS HIS SEAL

SEBACH HIS SEAL

THUREAL HIS SEAL

The Conjuration:
"I Conjure thee O Thou mighty & Potent Prince &c."

SYMIEL, HIS SEAL

The 14th Spirit in order [but the second under the Empire of the North] is called Symiel, who ruleth as King in the North & by East; who hath 10 Dukes to attend him in the day, and a 1000 for the night; & Every one of them hath a Certaine Number of servants whereof we shall make mention of the 10 that belong to the day; and 10 of those that belong to ye night; & those of the day are very good and not disobedient; as those of the night are, for they are stuborn, and will not Appear willingly, &c. Also those Dukes of the day hath 720 servants among them to do their will; & those 10 of the night hath 790 servants to attend on them as occasion serves:

The names of these 20 is as followeth; with their seals & numbers of servants, &c.

THE 10 THAT ARE UNDER SYMIEL BELONGING TO YE DAY:

ASMIEL, HIS SEAL
60

LARAEL, HIS SEAL
60

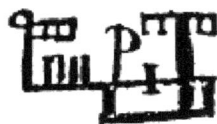

CHRUBAS, HIS SEAL
100

VAFROS, HIS SEAL
40

MALGRON, HIS SEAL
20

ROMIEL, HIS SEAL
80

ACHOT, HIS SEAL
60

BONIEL, HIS SEAL
90

DAGIEL, HIS SEAL
100

MUSOR, HIS SEAL
110

SYMIEL, HIS SEAL

THE 10 FOLLOWING BELONG TO THE NIGHT.

MAFRUS, HIS SEAL
70

MARIANU, HIS
SEAL
100

APIEL, HIS SEAL
30

NARZAD, HIS SEAL
20

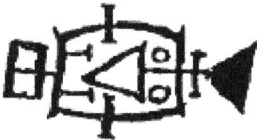

CURIEL, HIS SEAL
40

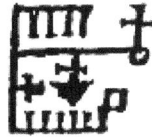

MURAHE, HIS SEAL
30

MOLAEL, HIS SEAL
10

RICHEL, HIS SEAL
120

ARAFES, BIS SEAL
50

MALAD, HIS SEAL
130

The Conjuration:
"I Conjure thee O thou Mighty & Potent Prince; &c."

ARMADIEL, HIS SEAL

The 15th. Spirit in order [but the 3rd. under the Empire of the North] is called Armadiel, who ruleth as King in the North East Part; and hath many Dukes under him, besides other servants; where of we shall make mention of 15, or the Chiefe Dukes, which hath 1260 servants to attend them; these Dukes are to be called in the day & night, dividing the same into 15 parts; beginning at Sunrise with the first Spirit, & so on till you come to the last Spirit & the last division of the Night; these Spirits are all good by nature; & willing to do your will in all things; these be their Names & seals; &c.

ALFERIEL, HIS SEAL

IAZIEL, HIS SEAL

ORARIEL, HIS SEAL

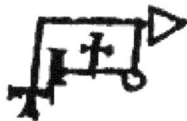

PANDIEL, HIS SEAL

ORIN, HIS SEAL

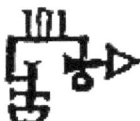

CARASIBA, HIS SEAL

SAMIEL, HIS SEAL

MASSAR HIS SEAL

PARABIEL, HIS SEAL

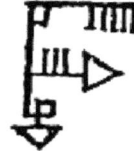

ASMAEL, HIS SEAL

LAIEL, HIS SEAL

CALUARNIA, HIS SEAL

ASBIBIEL, HIS SEAL

MAFAYR, HIS SEAL

OENIEL, HIS SEAL

The Conjuration:
"I Conjure thee O thou Mighty & Potent Prince Armadiel; &c."

BARUCHAS HIS SEAL

The 16th. Spirit in order [but the 4th. under the Empire of the North] is called Baruchas, who ruleth as King in the East & by North; & hath many Dukes and other servants to Attend him; Whereof we shall make mention of 15 of the Chief Dukes; that belong to the day and night, who hath 7040 servants to attend on them; they are all by nature good; and are willing to obey; &c. You are to call these Spirits in the same manner as is showed in the foregoing Experiment of Armadiel; and his Dukes, that is in Dividing the day & night into 15 parts; &c.

THE NAMES & SEALS OF THESE 15 (DUKES) IS AS FOLLOWETH:

BUITA (QUITA), HIS SEAL

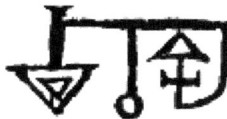

BAOXAS, HIS SEAL

SARAEL, HIS SEAL

GERIEL, HIS SEAL

MELCHON, HIS SEA

CAUAYR, HIS SEAL

ABOC, HIS SEAL

CARTAEL, HIS SEAL

IANIEL, HIS SEAL

PHAROL, HIS SEAL

MONAEL, HIS SEAL

CHUBOR, HIS SEAL

LAMAEL, HIS SEAL

DORAEL, HIS SEAL

DECANIEL, HIS SEAL

The Conjuration:
"I Conjure thee O thou Mighty & Potent Prince Baruchas; &c."

THE WANDERING PRINCES

In this place we are to give you the understanding of all the Mighty and Potent Princes; with their servants, which wandereth up & downe in the Ayre & never Continueth in one place; &c.

THE SEAL OF GERADIEL

Whereof of one of the Chiefe & first is Called Geradiel; who hath 18150 servants to attend him; for he hath no Dukes nor Princes; -- Therefore he is to be invocated Alone; but when he is called, there comes a great number of his servants with him; but more or less according to the hour of the day or night he is called in; for the 2 first hours of the day [according to the Planetary Motion] and the 2 second hours of the Night, there comes 470 of his servants with him; And in the 2 second hours of the day; & the 2 third hours of the night there comes 500 of his servants with him; & in the 2 third hours of the day and the 2 fourth hours of the night there comes 930 of his servants with him; and in the 2 fourth hours of the day; & the 2 fifth hours of the night there comes 1560 of his servants; &c and the 2, 5th. hours of the day, and the 2, 6th. hours of the night there comes 13710 of his servants, & in the 2 sixth or last hours of the day there comes 930 servants; & in the first 2 hours of the night there comes 1560 of his servants, &c. They are all indifferent good by nature, and will obey in all things willingly; &c.

The Conjuration:

"I Conjure thee O thou Mighty and Potent prince Geradiel, who wandereth here and there in the Ayre; with thy servants; I Conjure ye Geradiel that thou, forthwith Appeare with thy Attendants in this first hour of the day -- here before Me in this Crystal Stone, &c.".

THE NAME & SEAL OF BURIEL

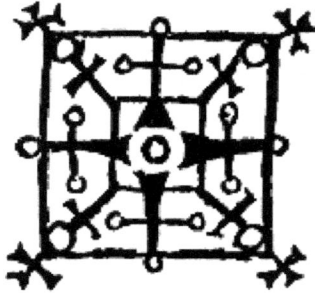

The next of these wandering Princes is called Buriel; who hath many Dukes and other Servants, which Doth Attend on him to doe his will, they are all by nature evil; and are hated by all other Spirits; they Appear Rugish; & in the forme of a Serpent with a Virgins head; and Speaketh with a mans voyce, they are to be called in the night, and in the Planetary hours, whereof wee shall mention 12 of the Chiefe Dukes that answereth to the 12 Planetary hours in the night; who hath 880 servants to Attend on them in the night; Their Names and Seals are as followeth; &c.

THE 12 DUKES ARE AS FOLLOWETH:

MEROSIEL HIS SEAL

NEDRIEL, HIS SEAL

ALMADIEL, HIS SEAL

FUTIEL, HIS SEAL

CUPRIEL, HIS SEAL

DRUSIEL, HIS SEAL

BUSIIEL, HIS SEAL

CARMIEL, HIS SEAL

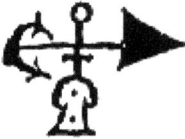

SARUNIEL, HIS SEAL

DRUBIEL, HIS SEAL

CASBRIEL, HIS SEAL

NASTROS, HIS SEAL

The Conjuration:
"I Conjure thee O thou Mighty and Potent prince Buriel, who
wandereth here and there in the Ayre; with thy Dukes & other (of)

thy servant Spirits; -- I Conjure thee Buriel that thou forthwith Appear with thy Attendents in this first hour of the night, here before me in this Crystal Stone [or here before this Circle] in a faire and Comely Shape, to do my will in all things that I shall desire of you; &c."

HIDRIEL HIS SEAL

The 3rd. of these wandring Princes is Called Hidriel, who hath 100 Great Dukes besides 200 Lesser Dukes; & servants without number; whereof we shall mention 12 of the Chiefe Dukes who hath 1320 servants to Attend them; they are to be called in the day, as well as in the night Accordingly to the Planetary Motion; the first beginneth with the first hour of the day or night; and so successively on; till you come to the last; they appear in the forme of a Serpent with a Virgins head & face; yet they are very courteous and willing to obey; they delight most in or about waters; & all Moyst Grounds; &c. Their Names & Seals are as followeth:

MORFATIEL, HIS SEAL

SAMIEL, HIS SEAL

CHALMORIEL, HIS SEAL

DUSIRIEL, HIS SEAL

PESARIEL, HIS SEAL

CHAMIEL, HIS SEAL

MUSUZIEL, HIS SEAL

ARBIEL, HIS SEAL

LAMENIEL, HIS SEAL

LUSIEL, HIS SEAL

BRACKIEL, HIS SEAL

CHARIEL, HIS SEAL

The Conjuration:
"I Conjure thee O thou Mighty and Potent Prince; &c."

PIRICHIEL, HIS SEAL

The 4th, in order of these wandring Princes is called Pirichiel; he hath no Princes nor Dukes; but Knights; whereof we shall mention 8 of the Chiefe; These being sufficient for practise; who hath 2000 servants under them; they are to be called According to the Planetary Motion; they are all good by nature and will do your will willingly, – their Names and Seals are as followeth:

DAMARSIEL, HIS SEAL

MENAZIEL, HIS SEAL

CARDIEL, HIS SEAL

DEMEDIEL, HIS SEAL

HURSIEL, HIS SEAL

ALMASOR, HIS SEAL
(OR ALMARIEL)

NEMARIEL, HIS SEAL   CUPRISIEL, HIS SEAL

The Conjuration:
"I Conjure thee; O thou Mighty & Potent Prince Pirichiel; who
wandreth, &c."

EMONIEL SEAL

The 5th. Wandring Spirit is called Emoniel, who hath one hundred Princes & Chief Dukes besides 20 under Dukes & a multitude of servants to attend them, whereof we shall mention 12 of the Chief Princes or Dukes who hath 1320 (under) Dukes & other inferior Spirits to Attend them, they are all by nature good & willing to obey. And they are to be called in the day as well as in the night & according to the Planetary order, it is so they inhabit mostly in woods, their names & seals are as followeth:

ERMENIEL SEAL

VASENEL SEAL

PANUEL SEAL

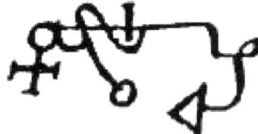

MASINEL SEAL

CRUHIEL SEAL

EDRIEL SEAL

CARNODIEL SEAL

DRAMIEL SEAL

PANDIEL SEAL

ARMISIEL SEAL

CASPANIEL SEAL

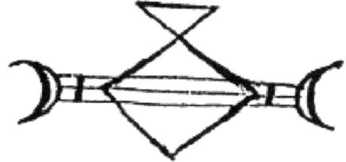

MUSINIEL SEAL

The Conjuration:
"I Conjure thee O thou Mighty & Potent Prince Emoniel, who wanderest, &c."

ICOSIEL HIS SEAL

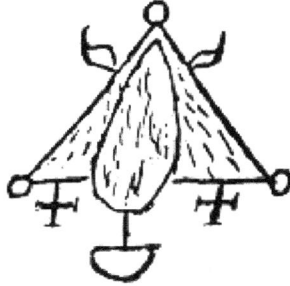

The 6th. of these Wandring Princes is Called Icosiel, who hath 100 Dukes & 300 Companions besides other servants which are more inferior, whereof we have taken 15 of the Chief Dukes for practise they being sufficient & they have 2000 &c. servants to attend on them, they are all of a good nature & will do what they are commanded, they appear mostly in houses because they delight most there, they are called in the 24 hours of the day & night, that is to divide the 24 hours into 15 parts according to the number of spirits, beginning at the first (spirit) at Sun Rise & with the last (spirit) at Sun Setting next day, Their Names & seals are as followeth &c.

MACHARIEL SEAL

TIANABRIEL SEAL

PSICHIEL SEAL

ZACHARIEL SEAL

TLANATIEL SEAL

ZOSIEL SEAL

ACAPSIEL SEAL

LERPHIEL SEAL

HERACIEL SEAL

AMODIEL SEAL

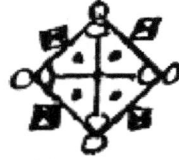
NATHRIEL SEAL

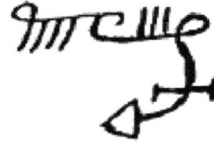
ATHESIEL SEAL

VRBANIEL SEAL

CUMARIEL SEAL

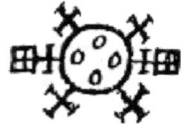
MUNETIEL SEAL

The Conjuration:
"I Conjure thee O thou Mighty & Potent Prince Icosiel, &c."

SOTERIEL HIS SEAL

The 7th. Spirit of these (that wander in the air) is called Soteriel, who hath under his command 200 Dukes & 200 Companions who changeth every year their places, they have many to Attend them, they are all good & very obedient, & here we shall mention twelve of the Chief Dukes, whereof the first 6 one year & the other 6 the year following, & so ruleth in order to serve their Prince; who hath under them 1840 servants to attend on them, they are to be called in the day as well as in the night, according to the Planetary Motion, their names & seals are as followeth &c.

INACHIEL SEAL

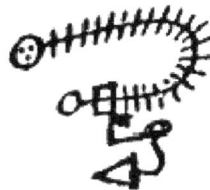

AMRIEL SEAL (AINOEL)

PROXEL SEAL

PRASIEL SEAL

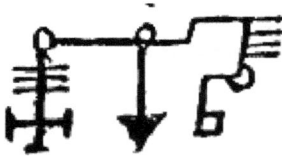

MARUCHA SEAL

AXOSIEL SEAL

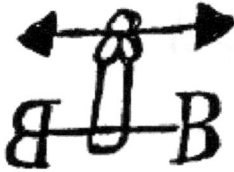

AMODAR SEAL

CAROEL SEAL

NADIUSIEL SEAL

MURSIEL SEAL

COBUSIEL SEAL

PENADER SEAL

The Conjuration:
"I Conjure thee O thou Mighty and Potent Prince, &c."

MENADIEL HIS SEAL

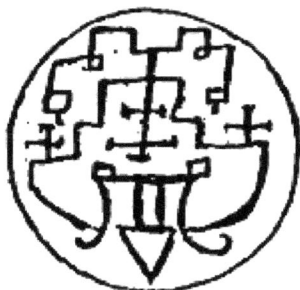

The 8th. of these Wandring Princes is called Menadiel, who hath 20 Dukes & a Hundred Companions & many other Servants, they being all of a good nature & very obedient, here we have mentioned 6 of the Chief Dukes & 6 of the Under Dukes who have 300 servants that attend them & note that you must call these according to the Planetary Motion, a Duke in the first hour & a Companion in the next, & so successively on all the hours of the day & night, whose names & seals followeth, &c.

THE DUKES   THE UNDER DUKES

LARMEL, HIS SEAL

BARCHIEL SEAL

BRASSIEL SEAL

ARMASIEL SEAL

CHAMOR SEAL

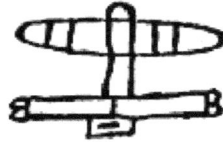

BARUCH SEAL

BENADIEL SEAL

NEDRIEL SEAL

CHARSIEL SEAL

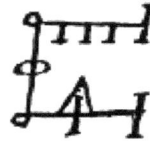

CURAIJN SEAL

SAMIEL SEAL

THARSON SEAL

The Conjuration:
"I Conjure thee O thou Mighty or Potent Prince Menadiel, &c."

MACARIEL HIS SEAL

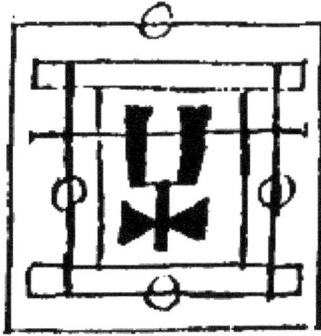

The 9th. Wandring Spirit in order is called Macariel, who hath 40 Dukes besides other inferior servants to attend him, whereof we shall mention 12 of the Chief Dukes which hath 400 servants to Attend them, they are all good by nature and obedient to do the will of the Exorcist, they appear in diverse forms but mostly in the form of a dragon with a virgins head, and these Dukes are to be called in the day as well as in the night, according to the Planetary order, & their names & seals are as followeth, &c.

CHANIEL SEAL

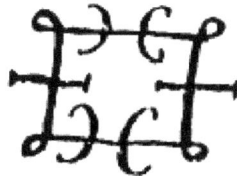

NAUSTUEL SEAL

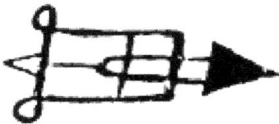

DRUSIEL SEAL

VERPIEL SEAL

ANDRAS SEAL

GERMEL SEAL

CAROEL SEAL

THIRSIEL SEAL

AMADIEL SEAL

BURFIEL SEAL

REMIJEL SEAL

AROMUSIJ SEAL

The Conjuration:
"I Conjure thee O thou Mighty & Potent Prince Macariel who
(Wandreth), &c."

VRIEL HIS SEAL

The 10th. Wandring Spirit in order is called Vriel, who hath 10 Dukes & 100 under Dukes with many servants to attend him, they are all by nature Evil & will not obey willingly & are very false in their doings, they appear in the form of a serpent with a virgins Head & face, whereof we shall mention but 10 of the Chief Dukes which hath 650 Companions and servants to attend them, their names & seals are as followeth &c.

CHABRI SEAL

DRAGON SEAL

DARBOS SEAL

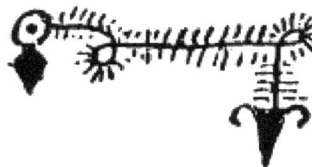

CURMIS SEAL

NARMIEL SEAL

DARPIOS SEAL

FRASMIEL SEAL

HERMON SEAL

BRYMIEL SEAL

ADRNSIS SEAL

The Conjuration:
"I Conjure thee O thou Mighty & Potent Prince Vriel, &c."

BYDIEL SEAL

The 11th & last Spirit & Prince of this Wandring order is called Bydiel, who hath under his command 20 Chief Dukes & 200 other Dukes more inferior besides very many servants, these Dukes changeth every year their office & place, they are all good & willing to obey the Exorcist in all things, they appear very beautiful in human shape, whereof we shall mention 10 of the Chief Dukes who have 2400 servants to attend them, their Names & Seals are as followeth &c.

MUDRIEL SEAL

CHAROBIEL SEAL

CRUCHAM SEAL

ANDRUCHA SEAL

BRAMSIEL SEAL

MANASAEL SEAL

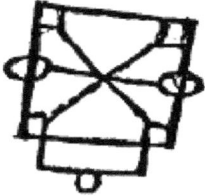

ARMONIEL SEAL

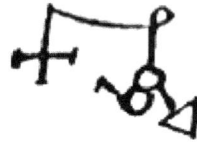

PERSIFIEL SEAL

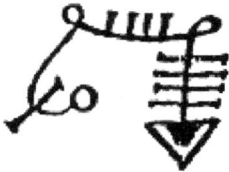

LEMONIEL SEAL

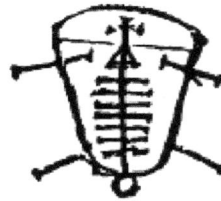

CHREMO SEAL

See conjuration that follows:

THE CONJURATIONS APPROPRIATE TO EACH RANK

THE CONJURATION OF THE WANDRING PRINCES:

"I Conjure thee O thou Mighty & Potent Prince Bydiel, who wanderest here & there in the Air, with thy Dukes & other (of) thy servants Spirits, I Conjure thee Bydiel that thou forthwith appear with thy Attendance (Attendants), in this first hour of the day, here before me in this Crystal Stone [or here before this Circle] in a fair and comely shape to do my will in all things that I shall desire of you..." Note this mark: in the Conjuration following & go on (from) there as it followeth.

THE CONJURATION OF THE PRINCES THAT GOVERN THE POINTS OF THE COMPASS:

"I Conjure thee O thou Mighty & Potent Prince Pamersiel, who ruleth as (a) King in the Dominion of the East under the Great Emperer Carnatiel, I Conjure thee Pamersiel that you forthwith appear with thy attendents in this first hour of the day, here before me in this Crystal Stone [or here before this circle] in a fair & comely shape to (do) my will in all things that I shall desire of you..." & observe this (mark) in the Conjuration (that follows) and go on as followeth.

THE CONJURATION OF THE 4 EMPIRES (EMPERORS):

"I Conjure thee O thou great & Mighty & Potent Prince Carnatiel who is the the Emperor & Chief King Ruling in the Dominion of the East, I Conjure (thee) Carnatiel that thou forthwith appear..." & observe this mark & go on (from) there in the following Conjuration.

THE CONJURATION TO THE WANDRING DUKES, HOW TO CALL THEM FORTH AND ANY OTHER DUKES THAT DOTH NOT WANDER, ONLY LEAVING OUT [WANDERING HERE & THERE (IN THE AIR)] AND ONLY FOR (THE) PRINCE SAY DUKE:

"I Conjure thee O thou Mighty & Potent Duke N, who wanderest here & there with thy Prince N, & other (of) his & thy servants in the Air, I Conjure thee N that thou forthwith appear.." & note this mark & go on (from) there in the following Conjuration.

THE CONJURATION OF THOSE DUKES THAT DO NOT WANDER BUT BELONG TO THE PRINCES THAT GOVERN THE POINTS OF THE COMPASS:

"I Conjure thee O thou Mighty Duke N, Who rulest under the Prince or King N, in the Dominion of the East, I Conjure thee N, that thou appear forthwith alone or with thy servants, in this first [or second] hour of the day, here before me in this Crystal Stone [or before this Circle] in a fair & comely shape to do my will in all things that I shall desire or request of you. I conjure & powerfully command you N by him that said the word & it was done & by all the holy & powerful names of God who is the only Creator of Heaven and Earth and Hell & what is Contained in them, Adonay, El, Elohim, Elohe, Elion, Escerchi, Zebaoth, Jah, Tetragram-maton Sadai, the only Lord God of hosts, that you forthwith appear unto me here in this Crystal Stone [or here before this Circle] in a fair & comely Human shape without hurt to me or any other Creature that the great God Jehovah hath Created & made, and come ye peaceably, visibly and affably without delay Manifesting what I desire, being conjured by the name of the Eternal Living true God Heliorin Tetragrammaton Anepheneton & fulfill my Commands & Persist unto the end, I conjure, Command & Constrain you Spirit N by Alpha & Omega & by the name Primeumaton which commandeth the Whole Host of heaven & by all these names which Moses named when he by the power of these names brought great plagues upon Pharaoh & all the people of Egypt; Zebaoth, Escerchie, Oriston, Elian, Adonay primeumaton, & by the name Schersieta Mathia which Joshua called upon the Sun stayed its course; & by the Hagioss & by the Seal of Adonay, & by

Agla on Tetragrammaton to whom all creatures are obedient & by the dreadful Judgement of the most high God & by the holy Angels of heaven & by the mighty wisdom of the omnipotent God of hosts that you come from all parts of the world & make rational Answers to all things that I shall ask of you & come ye peaceably & visibly & affably speaking to me with a voice intelligible & to my understanding, therefore come ye, come ye,in the name of Adonay Zebaoth, Adonay Aamioram, come, why stay ye, hasten Adonay Saday the King of Kings Commands you." ----

When he appears, show him the seal & pentacle of Solomon saying, "Behold the Pentacle of Solomon which I have brought before your presence..." as it is showed in the first book Goetia at the latter end of the Conjurations, also when you have had your desire of the Spirit, license him to depart as is showed there in the book Goetia, &c.

SO ENDETH THE SECOND BOOK CALLED THEURGIA GOETIA

THE ART PAULINE

Here beginneth ye Book called the Art Pauline of Solomon the King, & this is divided into two parts, the first the Angels of the Hours of the Day & Night, the second the Angels of the signs of the Zodiack, as hereafter followeth. The nature of the 24 Angels of the Day & Night changeth every day & their offices is to do all things that is attributed to the 7 Planets but that changeth every day also, as for example, you may see in the following treatise is that the Angel Samael ruleth the first hour of the day beginning at Sun Rising, supposing it to be on a Monday, in the first hour of the day that is attributed to the Moon, and you call Samael or any of his Dukes, their offices in that hour is to do all things that is attributed to the Moon but if you call him or any of his servants Dukes on a Tuesday morning at Sunrising being the first hour of the Day their offices is to do all things that is attributed to Mars & so the like rule is to be observed in the first hour of every day & the like is to be observed of the Angels & their servants that ruleth any of the other hours either in the Day or Night, also again there is an observation (rule) to be observed in making the seals of the 24 Angels, according to the time of the year, day and hour that you call the Angel or his servants in to do your will, but you cannot mistake therein if you do but observe the example that is laid down in the following work, they being all fitted for the tenth day of March, being on a, Wednesday in the year 1641 according to the old account. To know what is attributed to the 7 Planets, I do refer you to the books of Astrology whereof large volumes hath been written. When the seal is made according to the former directions, lay it upon the Table of Practice, upon that part of the Table that it notes with the Character that the Lord of the Ascendant is of, lay your hand on the seal & say the Conjuration that is at the latter end of this third part for it serves of all, only changing the names according to the time you work.

The table of Practise

239

The perfume is to be made of such things as is attributed to the 7 Planets, &c. ♂ is the lord of the Ascendant of every first hour of the day whilst the Sun goes through Aries & Scorpio, so is the ♀ Ascendant every first hour whilst the ☉ goes through ♉ & ♎ so the like of the rest.

THE 24 HOURS OF THE DAY & NIGHT

The first hour of the day is ruled by an Angel called **Samael**, who hath under his command many Dukes & servants whereof we shall mention **8** of the Chief Dukes which is sufficient for practise, who hath 444 servants to attend them, their names are as followeth (viz) **Ameniel, Charpon, Darosiel, Monasiel, Brumiel, Nestoriel, Chremas, Meresyn**; now to make a seal for any of these 8 Dukes or their Chief Prince **Samael**, do as followeth, first write the character of the Lord of the Ascendant, secondly the Moon afterwards the rest of the Planets; after that the Characters & Sign that ascends upon the 12th. house in that hour, as it shows in the Sigil following, which is fitted for the 10th. day of March, in the year of our Lord 1641, being on a Wednesday & the first hour of the Day.

The 2nd. hour of the day is called **Sovormi**, and the Angel that governs this hour is called **Anael**, who hath 10 chief Dukes to attend him, whereof we shall make mention of 9, but the 3 first are of the Chief & the other 6 are of the under Dukes. They have 330 servants to attend them. These 9 are as followeth: **Menerches, Sarchiel, Cardiel, Orphiel, Elmoijm, Ruosiel, Ermosiel, Granijel.** & when you have a desire to work in the second hour of Wednesday on the 10th. day of March make a seal before on clean paper or parchment, writing first the character of the Lord of the Ascendant, then the rest of the planets & the Sign of the 12th. house as you see it in the Sigil. & when it is made, lay it on that part of the Table that hath the same Character as the Lord of the Ascendant is. Observe this rule in all the following part, you cannot err. Then say the Conjuration at the latter end.

The 3rd. hour of the day is called Danlor, & the Angel thereof is called Veguaniel, who hath 20 Chief Dukes & 200 lesser & a great many servants to attend them, whereof we shall mention 4 of the Chief Dukes & 8 of the lesser Dukes who hath 1700 servants to attend them. Their names are as followeth: Ansmiel, Persiel, Mursiel, Zoetiel, Drelmech, Sadimel, Parniel, Comadiel, Gemary, Xautiel, Serviel, Euriel, these being sufficient for practice. Make a seal suitable to the day & hour of the year, as this is for the time before mentioned, & you cannot Err. Then say the Conjuration.

The 4th. hour of the day is called Elechin & the Angel that ruleth that hour is called Vachmiel, who hath 10 Chief Dukes & 100 under Dukes besides many servants, whereof we shall mention 5 of the Chief Dukes & 10 of the under Dukes, who hath 155 servants to attend them. Their names are as followeth: Ammiel, Larmiel, Martfiel, Ormijel, Zantiel, Emertiel, Permiel, Queriel, Serubiel, Daniel, Fermiel, Thuzez, Vaaesiel, Zasviel, Harmiel, they being sufficient for practise. Make a seal suitable for this hour as before directed, & you cannot err. The form of it will be as this is here for the time before mentioned & when it is made, do as you were before directed. Then say the Conjuration.

The 5th. hour of every day is called Tealeach & the Angel ruling it is called Sasquiel, he hath 10 Chief Dukes & 100 lesser Dukes & many servants, whereof we shall mention 5 of the Chief & 10 of the lessor Dukes who hath 5550 servants to attend them. Their names are (viz): Damiel, Aramiel, Maroch, Serapiel, Putrsiel Jameriel, Futuniel, Ramesiel, Amisiel, Omezach, Lameros, Zathiel, Fustiel, Bariel, being sufficient for practise. Then make a seal suitable for the time, as I have here given you an example of, for the Day aforesaid & year 1641. When you have made it, lay it upon the table as you were before directed & say the Conjuration.

The 6th. hour of the day is called Genphorim, & the Angel ruling that hour is called Samiel, who hath 10 Chief Dukes & 100 lesser Dukes besides many other inferior servants, whereof we shall mention 5 of the Chief Dukes & 10 of the lesser, who hath 5550 servants to attend them. Their names are these (viz): Arnebiel, Charuch, Medusiel, Nathmiel, Pemiel, Jamiel, Jenotriel, Sameon, Trasiel, Zamion, Nedaber, Permon, Brasiel, Comosiel, Enader, these being sufficient for practise in this hour of the day. Then make a seal suitable to the time of the year, day & hour as I have made one for the time aforesaid, then lay it on the table as you was before directed & you cannot err. Then say the Conjuration.

The 7th. hour of the day is called Hemarim, & the Angel governing the same is called Banyniel, who hath 10 Chief Dukes & 100 under Dukes besides servants which are very many, whereof we shall make mention of 5 of the Chief Dukes & 10 of the lesser who hath 600 servants to attend them in this hour. Their names are these [viz:] Abrasiel, Nestori, Namiel, Sagiel, Harmiel, Naustrus, Varmay, Thusrnas, Crosiel, Pastiel, Venesiel, Enarisn, Dusiel, Kathos, they being sufficient for practise in this hour, & then make a seal as I give you here an example. Then lay it on the table as you were before directed & having all things in readiness, say the Conjuration.

The 8th. hour of the day is called Jenamin, & the Angel that governs the same is called Osmadiel, who hath 10 Chief Dukes & 100 lessor Dukes besides many other servants, whereof we shall make mention of 5 of the Chief Dukes & 10 of the lesser who hath 3100 servants to attend them, they being sufficient for practise. Their names are (viz) Serfiel, Amatim, Chroel, Mesiel, Lantrhes, Demaros, Janosiel, Larfuti, Vemael, Thribel, Mariel, Remasin, Theoriel, Framuin, Ermiel, & then make a seal for the 8th. hour as is showed by this seal which is made for an example. Then lay it on the table & say the Conjuration.

The 9th. hour of the day is called Carron & the Angel ruling it is called Uvadriel, who hath many Dukes both of the greater & lesser order, besides many other servants which are more inferior, whereof 10 of the greater & 100 of the lesser Dukes hath 192980 servants in order to obey & serve them, whereof we shall mention the names of 5 of greater Dukes & 10 of the lesser Dukes, who hath 650 Chief servants to attend on them in this hour, being sufficient for practise. Their names are these (viz) Astromiel, Charnis, Pamorij, Damiel, Madriel, Chromos, Menos, Brasiel, Nesarin, Zoijmiel, Trubas, Zarmiel, Lameson, Zasnoz, Janediel, & when you have a desire to make an experiment in this hour, make a seal as aforesaid, the form of this for an example & when it is made, lay it on the Table as aforesaid and then say the conjuration.

The 10th. hour in any day is called Lamathon & the Angel ruling it is called Oriel, who hath many Dukes & servants divided into orders which contains 5600 Spirits, whereof we shall mention 5 of the Chief Dukes & 10 of the next lesser Dukes who hath 1100 servants to attend on them. They being sufficient for practise. Their names are as followeth (viz) Armosy, Drabiel, Penaly, Mesriel, Choreb, Lemur, Ormas, Charny, Zazyor, Naveron, Xantros, Basilon [Basilion], Nameron, Kranoti, Alfrael. And when you have a desire to practice in this hour make a seal suitable to the time: as this hear is made for the 10th hour on Wednesday the 10th of march in the year 1641 it being for an example [sic] and when it is made lay it on the Table of practice: and say the conjuration.

The 11th. hour in any day is called Manelohim & the Angel governing this hour is called Bariel, who hath many Dukes & servants which are divided into 10 parts which contains 5600 Spirits, whereof we shall mention 5 of the Chief Dukes of the first order & 10 lesser Dukes of the second order, who hath 1100 to attend them, they being sufficient for practise. Their names are these (viz) Almarizel, Parlimiel, Chadros, Turmiel, Lamiel, Menafiel, Demasor, Omary, Hehuas, Zemoel, Ahuas, Perman, Comiel, Temas, Lanifiel, & then do all things in order as aforesaid &c.

The 12th. hour of every day is called Nahalon & the Angel governing this hour is called Beratiel, who hath many Dukes & other servants which is divided into 12 degrees, the which contain to the number of 3700 Spirits in all, whereof we shall make mention of 5 of the greater Dukes & 10 of the next order who hath a 1100 servants to attend them, they being sufficient for practise. Their names are these (viz) Camaron, Attrafrd2, Penatiel, Demarec, Famaris, Pamiel, Nerostiel, Emarson, Uvirix, Sameron, Edriel, Chorion, Romiel, Tenostiel, Uamary, & then make the seal & do as Aforesaid &c.

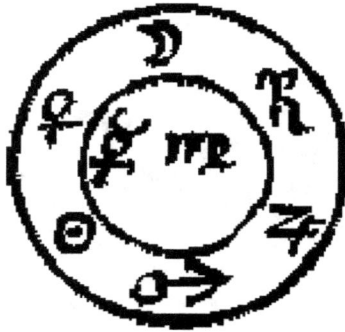

The first hour of every night is called Omalhavien, & the Angel ruling it is called Sabrachon, who hath 1540 Dukes & other servants which are divided into 10 orders or parts, whereof we shall mention 5 of the Chief Dukes & 10 of the next order, they being sufficient for practise. Their names are these (viz) Domaros, Amerany, Penoles, Mordiol, Nastul, Ramasiel, Omedriel, Frandedac, Charsiel, Darnason, Hayzoim, Enalon, Turtiel, Uvonel, Rimaliel. They have 200 servants to attend them. & then prepare your seal suitable to the time & do all things as you were before directed &c.

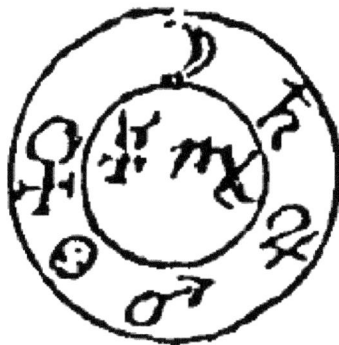

The second hour of any night is called Ponazur & the Angel ruling it is called Taktis, who hath 101550 Spirits to attend him, they being divided into 12 degrees or orders. Whereof we shall mention 6 of the Chief Dukes of the first order & 12 of the next, they being sufficient for practise. Their names are (viz) Almodar, Famoriel, Nedros, Ormozin, Chabril, Praxiel, Parmaz, Vomeroz, Emariel, Fromezin, Ramaziel, Granozy, Gabrynoz, Mezcoph, Tamariel, Venomiel, Janaziel, Zemizim. These have 1320 servants to attend them in this hour, to do their will. & when you will prepare your seal & do it in all things as before directed & you cannot err.

The 3rd. hour of every night is called Guabrion, and the Angel governing it is called Sarquamech, who hath 101550 Dukes & servants to attend him, which is divided into 12 degrees or orders, whereof we shall mention 6 Dukes of the first order & 12 of the second order, they being sufficient for practise. Their names are (viz) Monarim, Chrusiel, Penergoz, Amriel, Deminoz, Noztozoz, Evamiel, Sarmezyrs, Haylon, Uvabriel, Thurmytzol, Fromzon, Vanoir, Lemaron, Almonayzod, Janishyel, Mebrotzed, Zanthyozod. These have 1320 servants to attend them. & when you will make any experiment, make a seal proper to the time & do all things as aforesaid &c.

The 4th. hour of the night is called Ramersi, & the Angel governing it is called Jdfischa. He hath 101550 Dukes to attend & other servants (which) are divided into orders or degrees to attend him, whereof we shall mention 6 of the Chief Dukes & 12 of those Spirits of the second order, they being sufficient for practise. Their names are (viz) Armesiel, Iudoruan, Manoij, Lozor, Mael, Phersiel, Remozyn, Raisiel, Gemezin, Frosmiel, Haymayzod, Gapuviel, Jasphiel, Lamodiel, Adroziel, Zodrel, Bromiel, Coreziel, Etnatriel. These have 7260 servants to attend them. & when you have a desire to make an experiment, make your seal & do as aforesaid, &c.

The 5th. hour of every night is called Sanayfor and its Angel is called Abasdashon. He (has) 101550 Dukes & other servants at his command, they being divided 12 degrees or orders, whereof we shall mention 12 of the Dukes belonging to the first order & as many of the second, they being sufficient for practise in this hour. Their names are as followeth (viz) Moniel, Charaby, Appinel, Dematron, Necorin, Hameriel, Vulcamiel, Semelon, Clemary, Venesear, Samerin, Zantropis, Herphatzal, Chrymos, Palrozin, Nameten, Baymasos, Phaytiel, Neszomy, Uvesalor, Carmax, Vinariel, Kralina, Habalon, who hath 2400 servants to attend them. Then make your seal according to the time when you go to make an experiment & do all things as aforesaid, & you cannot err.

The 6th. hour of the night is called Thaasoron and the Angel governing it is called Zaazenach, who hath 101550 Dukes & other servants to attend him, they being divided into 12 orders, whereof we shall mention 12 of the Chief Dukes in the first order & 6 of the second order, they being sufficient for practise in this hour. Their names are these (viz) Amonzij, Menoyik, Pronestix, Ivamendor, Chorahol, Dramazod, Tuberiel, Humaziel, Lenaziel, Lamerotzod, Xerphiel, Zeziel, Pammon, Dracon, Gemetzol, Gnaviel, Rudozer, Satmon, who hath 2400 servants to attend them, when you go to work, make your seal & do all things as before directed.

The 7th. hour of the night is called Venador & its Angel is called Mendrion, who hath 101550 Dukes & other servants to attend him, they being divided into 12 orders, whereof we shall mention 12 of the first Chief Dukes & 6 of the next order, they being sufficient for practise. Their names are (viz) Mumiel, Choriel, Genaritzos, Poudroz, Memesiel, Someriel, Ventariel, Zachariel, Dubraz, Marchiel, Jonadriel, Pomoniel, Rayziel, Fornitzod, Amapion, Imonyel, Framoch, Machmag, who hath 1860 servants to attend them, when you intend to work, make your seal proper to the time, day & hour, & do all other things as you were before directed.

The 8th. hour of every night is called Ximalim & the Angel ruling is called Narcriel, who hath 101550 Dukes & other servants to attend him, being divided into 12 degrees, whereof we shall mention 12 Dukes on the first order & 6 of the next, they being sufficient for practise in this hour. Their names are (viz): Cambiel, Nedarim, Astrecon, Marifiel, Dramozin, Lustision, Amolzom, Lemozar, Xernisiel, Kanorfiel, Bufanotzod, Jamodroz, Xanoriz, Pastrion, Thomax, Hobrazim, Zimeloz, Gramsiel, who hath 30200 servants to attend them. When you intend to work, make your seal to this hour as this example is, and do as aforesaid.

The 9th. hour is called Zeschar & the Angel ruling is called Pamiel. He hath 101550 Dukes & other servants to attend him (which) are divided into 12 hours, whereof we shall mention 18 of the Chief Dukes. Their names are (viz) Demnnameals, Adyapon, Chermel, Fenadross, Vemasiel, Crnary, Matiel, Xenoroz, Brandiel, Evandiel, Jamriel, Befranzij, Jachoroz, Xanthir, Armapi, Orucas, Saraiel, who hath 1320 servants to attend them. When you intend to work in this hour of the night make a seal proper to the time & do all things else as you were before directed.

The 10th. hour (of the night) is called Malcho & the Angel governing it is called Iasgnarim, which hath 100 chief Dukes & 100 lesser Dukes, besides many other servants whereof we shall mention 6, three of the first & three of the second order, who hath 1628 servants to attend them. Their names are (viz) Laphoriel, Emerziel, Nameroizod, Chameray, Hazariel, Vramiel. Then make a seal & do as you were directed in all things, &c.

The 11th. hour of the night is called Alacho, & the Angel governing it is called Dardariel, who hath many Dukes & servants, whereof we shall mention 14 of the Chief Dukes & 7 of the next lesser order, who hath 420 servants to attend them. They are all good & obey Gods laws, their names are (viz) Cardiel, Permon, Armiel, Nastoriel, Casmiros, Damoriel, Fumarel, Masriel, Hariaz, Damer, Alachus, Emeriel, Mavezoz, Alaphar, Hemas, Druchas, Carman, Elamiz, Iatrziul, Lamerly, Hamerytzod. & then make your seal proper to the time & do as aforesaid &c.

The 12th. hour of the night is called Xphan & the Angel governing it is called Sarandiel, who hath many Dukes & servants, whereof we shall mention 14 of the Chief & good Dukes & 7 of the next & second order, who hath 420 servants to attend on them. Their names are as followeth: Adomel, Damasiel, Ambriel, Meriel, Denaryzod, Etharion, Kbriel, Marachy, Chabrion, Nestorel, Zachriel, Naveriel, Damery, Namael, Hardiel, Nefrias, Irmanotzod, Gerdriel, Dromiel, Ladrotzod, Melanas. & when you desire to make an experiment, make a seal proper to this hour, observe the day & time of the year, and all other directions as aforesaid &c. Then say the Conjuration following &c.

THE CONJURATION:

O thou Mighty & potent Angel Samael, who rulest the first hour of the day, I the servant of the most high God, do Conjure & instruct thee in the name of the most high omnipotent & immortal God of Hosts Jehovah Tetragrammaton & by the name & in the name of that God that you owe obediency to, & by the head of your Hierarchy & by the seal of mark you are known in power by, & by the 7 Angels that stands before the Throne of God, & by the 7 Planets & their seals & characters & by the Angel that ruleth the sign of the 12th. house which now ascends in thy first hour, that you would be so graciously pleased to gird up yourself together & by divine permission to move & come from all parts of the world wheresoever you be & show thyself visibly & plainly in this crystal stone to the light of mine eyes, speaking with a voice intelligible & to my understanding, & that you would be favorably pleased that I may have thy familiar friendship & constant society both now and at all times when I shall call thee forth to visible appearance, to inform & direct me in all things that shall seem good & lawful unto the Creator & thee, O thou great & powerful Angel Samael I invocate Adjure Command & most powerfully call you forth from your orders & places of residence to visible appearance in & through these great & mighty incomprehensible Signall & divine name of the great God who wast, is & ever shall be, Adonay Zebaoth, Adonay Amioram, Hagios Aglaon Tetragrammaton & by & in the name Primeumaton which commandeth the whole host of heaven, whose power & virtue is most Effectual for the calling you forth & command you to transmit your rays perfectly to my sight & voice to my ears, in & through this Celestial Stone, that I may plainly see you & perfectly hear you speak unto me, therefore move O thou mighty & blessed Angel Samael, & by his present name of the great God Jehovah, & by the Imperial Dignity thereof, descend & show your self visibly & perfectly in a pleasant & comely form before me in this Crystal Stone to the sight of mine eyes, speaking with a voice intelligible to apprehension, declaring & accomplishing all my desires that I shall ask or require of you, both herein & whatsoever truth or thing also that is just & lawful before the presence of Almighty God the Giver of all good gifts, unto whom I beg that he would be graciously pleased to bestow upon me, O thou servant of mercy Samael, be thou therefore friendly unto me & do for me, as the servant of the most high God, so far as God shall give you power to perform, whereunto I move you both in power & presence to appear, that I may sing with thee his holy Angel O-Napa-ta-man halle-le-la-jah, Amen. But before you call any of the Dukes, you are to Invocate the Chief governing Angel that governs the hour of the day or night, as followeth: "O thou mighty & potent Angel Samael, who by the decree of the most high King of Glory, Ruler & governor of this first hour of the day, I, the servant of the Highest, do desire & intreat you in & by these 3 great & potent names of God: Agla On Tetragrammaton, & by the power & virtue thereof, to assist & help me in my affaires & by your power & authority to send & cause to come & appear unto me, all or any of those Angels that I shall call by name that are residing under your government, to instruct, help aid and assist in all such matters or things according to their office as I shall desire or request of him or them & that they may do for me as for the servant of the Highest, Amen." Then begin as followeth: "Thou mighty & potent Angel Ameniel, who is the first & principal Duke ruling by divine pearission under the great & potent Angel Samael, who is the first great & mighty Angel ruling the first hour of the day, (I) the servant of the most high God do conjure & invocate thee in the name of the most Omnipotent & immortal Lord God of Hosts Jehovah "... So on as before, at this mark in the conjuration of Samael (as aforesaid), and when the Spirit is come, bid him welcome, then ask your desire & when you have done, dismiss him according to the order of dismissing.

SO ENDETH THE FIRST PART OF THE 3RD BOOK CALLED PAULINE OF SOLOMON THE KING

15	Gadiel	Zegiel	Zagiil	Abiel	Abiel	Hovael	Datziel	Goziel	Goziel	Baajah	Baajah	Vahasah	♂
16	Khoel	Chadiel	Chadiel	Sagel	Magiel	Vaziel	Hokel	Dachiel	Dachiel	Cashiel	Gacniel	Zavael	l
17	Loviel	Tohiel	Tahoel	Madiel	Sadiel	Zachiel	Varziel	Hophiel	Hophiel	Damiel	Dashiel	Chaziel	l
18	Hazael	Javiel	Javiel	Ahiel	Ahoel	Chotiel	Zethel	Vajael	Vajael	Haajah	Haajah	Tachael	l
19	Gociel	Chaziel	Chazael	Lavael	Mukel	Tijel	Chongel	Zachiel	Zachiel	Vashiel	Vaniel	Jabael	iel
20	Botiel	Bachiel	Bachael	Maziel	Saziel	Jochiel	Tobiel	Chabiel	Chabiel	Zanael	Zashiel	Cajoal	ael
21	Giel	Gotiel	Gotiel	Achiel	Achiel	Cabiel	Jagiel	Tagiel	Tagiel	Chael	Chael	Bachiel	l
22	Dachael	Dajel	Dajoel	Sotiel	Matiel	Bagiel	Codiel	Jadiel	Jadiel	Tashiel	Taniel	Gabael	
23	Habiel	Hachael	Hachael	Majel	Goel	Gadiel	Bohel	Chael	Cahael	Jmojah	Jashiel	Dagiel	iel
24	Vagel	Vabiel	Vabiel	Achael	Achael	Dahiel	Sael	Baviel	Baviel	Ciajah	Ciajah	Hodiel	l
25	Zadiel	Zagiel	Zagiel	Sabiel	Mabiel	Hovael	Daziel	Gozael	Gozael	Boshael	Bomiel	Vahoiah	
26	Chael	Chadiel	Chadiel	Magiel	Sagiel	Vasiel	Hochiel	Dachael	Dachael	Gamiel	Gashiel	Zavael	iel
27	Tavael	Tohael	Tahiel	Adiel	Adiel	Zachiel	Vatiel	Hatiel	Hatiel	Daael	Daael	Chazael	el
28	Josel	Javael	Daiel	Sahiel	Mahiel	G?otiel	Zael	Vagael	Vadael	Hoshael	Homiel	Tachiel	l
29	Chiel	Chaziel	Hoziel	Moviel	Savael	Tazael	Choch-iel	Zachiel	Zahael	Vannel	Vashiel	Jalael	l
30	Heriel	Sachael	Vachael	Aziel	Aziol	Jachiel	Tohiel	Casiel	Chanel	Zaajah	Zaajah	Cajael	iel

♐ ♃	♑ ♄	♒ ♄	♓ ♃
Taliel	Chahel	Chamel	Lachiel
Jamael	Tomael	Tosael	Nohiel
Casiel	Jaajah	Jaajah	Sanael
Laugael	Casmel	Camiel	Gnasiel
Naph-adel	Lamajah	Lashiel	Pangael
Satziel	Naajah	Naajah	Tzophal
Gnakiel	Sasaial	Samael	Kphiel
Poriel	Gnamiel	Gnash-iel	Ratziel
Tzaugel	Paajah	Paajah	Taraziel
Kabiel	T<?>iel	Tzaniel	Mathiel
Rogael	Kiniel	Kahiel	Bongael
Tadiel	Riajah	Raajah	Gobiel
Gnahoel	Tashiel	Taniel	Dagiel
Bovael	Gonam-iel	Gonas-tiel	Hadiel

THESE BE THE 12 SEALS WHICH IS ATTRIBUTED TO THE 12 SIGNS AND THE 360 ANGELS AFORESAID

Make this seal of ♂ 1 ounce ☉ 2 Drams ♀ 2 scruples & melt them together when the ☉ enters the first degree ♈ on the day of ♂.

When the ☽ is in the 9 or 10 degree of ♈ make it or finish it. Make this seal of ♀ 1 ounce ♃ 1 Dram ♂ 1 Scruple ☉ 2 Drams & melt them together in the very point the ☉ enters ♉ & so finish it &c.

♊

Make this seal of ☉ 1 Dram, & ☽ 1 Dram; melt them together when the ☉ enters ♊ & make a lamen thereof when the ☽ is in ♌ or ♓.

♋

Make this seal of ☽ when the ☉ enters ♋ in the hour of ☽, she generating & in good Aspect.

♌

Make this seal when the ☉ enters ♌, of ☉. Then after, when ♃ is in ♓, engrave the first figure, and the other side when the ☽ is in ♓. It must not come to the fire but once when it is melted.

♍

Make this seal when the ☉ enters ♍, of ♀ 1 Dram ☉ 1 Ounce ☽ 2 Drams ♄ 1 Scruple & melt them on ☉ Day. Then after when ☿ is well aspected on his day, engrave the word & Characters you see in the figure.

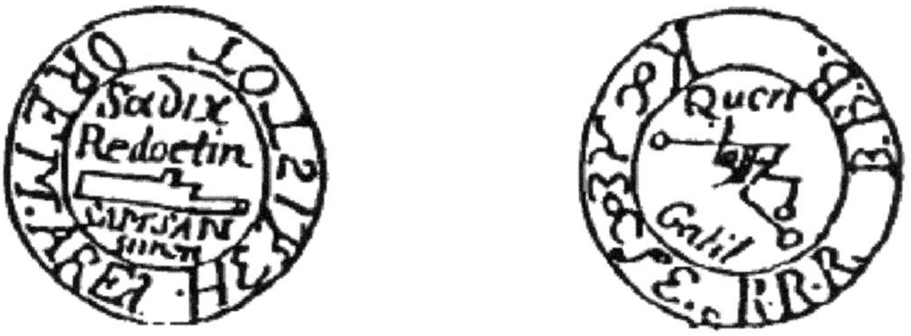

♎︎

Make this seal of ♀ melted & poured out & made when ☉ enters ♎.

♏︎

Make this seal when of ♂ on his day & hour when the ☉ enters ♏ & in that hour engrave the fore part of it. Afterward, when the ☉ enters ♈ engrave the other side.

♐

Make this seal when of pure ♃ in the hour of the ☉ enters ♐ & engrave it in the hour of ♃. This seal is to be hung in a Silver ring.

♑

Make this seal of ☉ & a ring of ♀ to hang it in when the ☉ enters ♑ & engrave it when ♄ is well aspected & in his day and hour.

Make this seal of ☉ 1 Ounce ♄ 2 Drams ♂ 1 Dram & melt them when the ☉ enters ♒ & engrave it as you see in this figure, when is in the ♄ 9th house.

Make this seal when the ☉ enters ♓, of ☉ ♂ ♀ & ☽, of each 2 Drams, of ♃ 1 scruple & let it be melted to engrave the same hour the ☉ enters ♓.

So when you know the Angel that governs the sign & degree of your Nativity & having the seal ready that belongs to that sign & degree as is showed before, then you are next to understand what order he is of, as is showed herein the following part.

First these genijs that belong to the Fiery Region, that is ♈♌ ♐ and governed by Michael thegreat Angel who is one of the Chief Messengers of God, who is toward the South, therefore these genijs are to be observed in the first hour of a Sunday & at the 8th. hour, also at the 3rd. & 10th. at night, directing yourself toward that quarter, they appear in Royal Apparel holding scepters in their hands, and riding on a Lyon or a Cock, their robes are of red & saffron color & most comely, they assume the shape Crowned Queen & very beautiful to behold.

Secondly these genijs that are attributed to ♉ ♍ & ♑ are of the Earthly Reigons & are governed by Vriel who hath 3 Princes to attend him (viz) Asaiel, Sochiel & Cassiel. Therefore the genijs that are Attributed to him & these signs are to be observed in the West. They appear like Kings, having green & silver robes, or like little children or women delighting in hunting, & they are to be observed on Saturday in the 1st. & 8th. hours of the day & the 3rd. & 10th. of the night, in those hours you are with privacy to obtain your desires directing yourself towards the west as aforesaid.

Thirdly those genijs that are attributed to ♊♎ & ♒ are of the Airy Region whose soverign is called Raphiel, who hath under him 2 princes called Seraphiel & Miel. Therefore these genijs are attributed to him & those signs are to be observed towards the East, on a Wednesday the 1st. hour of the day & 8th., at night the 3rd. & 10th. hours. They appear as Kings or beautiful young men in robes of diverse colors but mostly like women transcendently handsome by reason of their admirable whiteness & beauty.

Fourthly & lastly, these genijs that are attributed to ♋ ♏ & ♓ are of the Watery Regions & are governed by Gabriel who hath under him Samael, Madiel & Mael. Therefore these Genijs that are under these signs & are governed by Gabriel are to be observed on Mondays, towards the North at the 1st. & 8th. hours of the day & at night at the 3rd. & 10th. hours. They appear like Kings having green & silver robes or like little children or women delighting in hunting.

So in the next place, we are to observe the season of the year according to the constellations of the Celestial Bodies, otherwise we shall loose our labor, for if a genijs be of the Igneal Hierarchy its in vain to observe him in any other season but when the ☉ enters these signs which is of his nature, that is ♈ ♌ & ♐. So if it be a genij of the Earth, he is to be observed when the ☉ enters ♉♍ & ♑, & so the like in the rest. Otherwise thus: those genijs that are of the order of Fire are to be observed in the Summer Quarter & those of the Earth in Autumn, those of the Air in Spring, & those of the Water in Winter quarter. Their offices is to do all things that are just & lawful in the sight of the great God **Jehovah** & what is for our good & what shall concern the protection of our lives or beings or wellbeings & the doing good to our neighbors.

Now he that desireth to see his genius, ought to prepare himself accordingly. Now if his genius be of the fire his demands must be the consecration of his Body or person that he receives no hurt from or by any fire armes guns or the like and haveing a seal sutable, ready prepared, he is to weare it when he hath a desier to see his genius, That he may conferme it to him & for the time to come he may not fail of his assistance and protection at any time or occasion &c.

But if his genius be ayeriall [aerial] he reconcileth mens natures Increaseth love and affection between them causeth the deserved favour of kings and princes & secretly promoteth marriages: & Therefore he that hath such a genius before he observeth him should prepare a seal suitable to his order that he may have it confermed by him in the day and hour of observation, where of he shall see wonderfull & strange Effects and so the like of ye other 2 hierarchies: and when the time is come that you would see ye genius Turne yi face towards that quarter the signe is, and that with prayers to god: they being composed to your fancy, but sutable to ye matter in hand and there thou shalt find him; and haveing found him and sincerely acknowledged him doe your duty. Then will he, as being Benigne & sociable Illuminate your minde, takeing away all that is obscure & darke in the memory and make thee knowing in all sciences sacred & divine in an instant &c -- [Here followeth] a form of prayer which ought to be said upon that cost or quarter where the genius is several times, it being an Exorcisme to call the genius into the christall stone that is to stand upon the Table of practice before shewed, it being covered with a white linnen

THE CONJURATION OF THE HOLY GUARDIAN ANGEL

O thou great and blessed N. my angell guardian vouchsafe to descend from thy holy mansion which is Celestial, with thy holy Influence and presence, into this cristall stone, that I may behold thy glory; and enjoy thy society, aide and assistance, both now and for ever hereafter. O thou who art higer [higher] than the fortly [fourth] heaven, and knoweth the secrets of Elanel. Thou that rideth upon the wings of ye winds and art mighty and potent in thy Celestial and superlunary motion, do thou descend and be present I pray thee; and I humbly desiere and entreat thee. That if ever I have merited Thy socity [society] or if any of my actions and Intentions be real and pure & sanctified before thee bring thy external presence hither, and converse with me one of thy submissive pupils, By and in the name of [the] great god Jehovah, whereunto the whole quire [choir] of heaven singeth continualy: O Mappa la man Hallelujah. Amen.

SO ENDETH THE SECOND PART OF THE 3RD BOOK CALLED PAULINE OF SOLOMON THE KING
THE ART ALMADEL

Here Beginneth the The Fourth Part of this Book Which is called the Art Almadel of Solomon By this art Solomon attained great wisdom from the Chief Angels that govern the four Altitudes of the World: for you must observe that there are four Altitudes which represent the four Corners of the West, East, North and South: the which is divided into 12 parts; that is, every part 3. And the Angels of every one1 of these parts hath their particular virtues and powers, as shall be showed in the following matter &c. Make this Almadel of pure white wax; but the others must be coloured suitable to the Altitude. It is to be 4 inches square, and 6 inches over every way, and in every corner a hole, and write betwixt every hole with a new pen those words and names of God following. But this is to be done in the day and hour of Sol. Write upon the first part towards the East, ADONAIJ, HELOMI, PINE. And upon the second towards the South part HELION, HELOI, HELI. And upon the West part JOD, HOD, AGLA. And upon the Fourth part which is North write TETRAGRAMMATON, SHADAI, JAH. And betwixt the first and the other parts make the pentacle of Solomon thus: ⚝ , and betwixt the first quarter write this word ANABONA, and in the middle of the Almadel make a Sexangle figure ✳, and in the middle of it a triangle, wherein must be written these names of God HELL, HELION, ADONAIJ, and this last have round about the six-angled figure, as here it is made for an example. And of the same wax there must be made four candles. And they must be of the same colour as the Almadel is of. Divide your wax into three parts: one to make the Almadel of, and the other two parts to make the candles of. And let there come forth from every one of them a foot made of the same wax to support the Almadel. This being done, in the next place you are to make a seal of pure gold or silver (but gold is best) whereon must be engraved those three names HELION, HELLUION, ADONAIJ.

OF THE FIRST ALTITUDE IS CALLED CHORA ORIENTIS, OR THE EAST ALTITUDE.

And to make an experiment in this Chora it is to be done in the day and hour of the Sun. And the power and office of those angels is to make all things fruitful, and increase both animals and vegetables in creation and generation, advancing the birth of children, and making barren women fruitful. And their names are these, viz: ALIMIEL, GABRIEL, BARACHIEL, LEBES, HELISON. And note you must not pray for any angel but those that belong to the Altitude you have a desire to call forth. And when you operate set the four candles upon four candlesticks, but be careful you do not light them before you begin to operate. Then lay the Almadel between the four candles upon a waxen foot that comes from the candles, and lay the golden seal upon the Almadel, and having the invocation ready written upon virgin parchment, light the candles and read the invocation. And when he appeareth he appeareth in the form of an Angel carrying in his hand a banner or flag having the picture of a white cross1 upon it, his body being wrapped round with a fair cloud, and his face very fair and bright, and a crown of rose flowers upon his head. He ascends first upon the superscription on the Almadel, as it were a mist or fog. Then must the exorcist have ready a vessel of earth of the same colour as the Almadel is of, and the other of his furniture, it being in the form of a basin, and put thereinto a few hot ashes or coals, but not too much lest it should melt the wax of the Almadel. And put therein three little grains of mastick in powder so that it may fume and the smell go upwards through the holes of the Almadel when it is under it. And as soon as the Angel smelleth it he beginneth to speak with a low voice, asking what your desire is, and what you have called the princes and governors of this Altitude for.

HELION HELOI HELI

ANABONA

ADONAIJ HELOMI PINE

ANABONA

A

I

O

HELL
HELION
ADONAIJ

N

ANABONA

JOD HOD AGLA

ANABONA

TETRAGRAMMATON SHADAI JAH

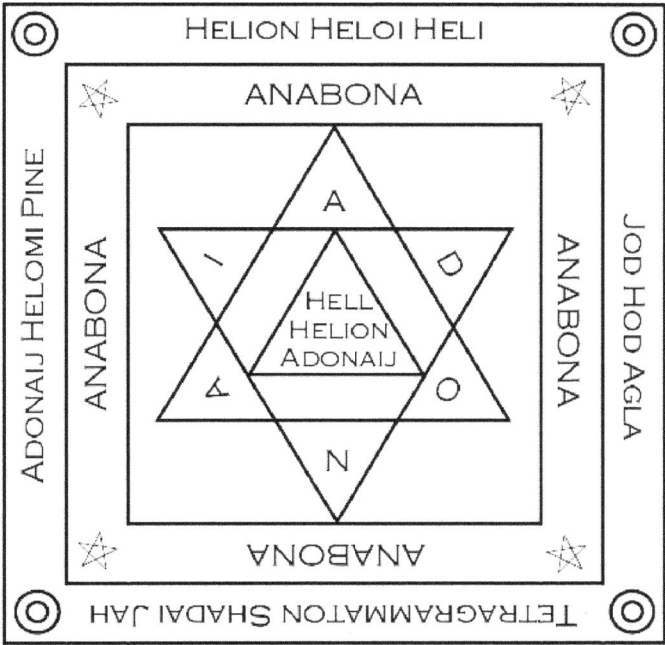

Then you must answer him, saying: I desire that all my requests may be granted and what I pray for may be accomplished: for your office maketh it appear and declareth that such is to be fulfilled by you, if it please God, Adding further the particulars of your request, praying with humility for what is lawful and just: and that thou shall obtain from him. But if he do not appear presently, then you must obtain the golden seal, and make with it three or four marks upon the candles, by which means the Angel will presently appear as aforesaid. And when the Angel departeth he will fill the whole place with a sweet and pleasant smell, which will be smelled for a long time. And note the golden seal will serve and is used in all the operations of all four Altitudes.

The colour of the Altitude belonging to the first Altitude, or Chora, is lilywhite; the second Chora a perfect red rose colour; the third Chora is to be a green mixed with a white silver colour; the fourth Chora is to be black mixt with a little green or a sad colour.

279

OF THE SECOND CHORA OR ALTITUDE

Note that the other three Altitudes, with their Signs and Princes can exert power over goods and riches, and can make any man rich or poor. And as the first Chora gives increase and maketh fruitful, so these give decrease and barrenness. And if any have a desire to operate in any of these three following Choras or Altitudes, they must do it in die Solis in the manner above showed. But do not pray for anything that is against God and His laws, but what God giveth according to the custom or course of nature: that you may desire and obtain. All the furniture to be used is to be of the same colour the Almadel is of. And the princes of the second Chora are named, viz: APHIRIZA, GENON, GERON, ARMON, GEREIMON. And when you operate kneel before the Almadel, with clothes of the same colour, in a closet hung with the same colours also; for the holy apparition will be of the same colours. And when he appeareth, put an earthen vessel under the Almadel, with fire or hot ashes and three grains of mastick to perfume as aforesaid. And when the Angel smelleth it he turneth his face towards you, asking the exorcist with a low voice why he hath called the princes of this Chora or Altitude. Then you must answer as before:

"I desire that my requests may be granted, and the contents thereof may be accomplished: for your office maketh it appear and declareth that such is to be done by you, if it please God."

And you must not be fearful, but speak humbly, saying:

"I recommend myself wholly to your office, and I pray unto you, Prince of this Altitude, that I may enjoy and obtain all things according to my wishes and desires."

And you may further express your mind in all particulars in your prayer, and do the like in the two other Choras following. The Angel of the second Altitude appeareth in the form of a young child with clothes of a satin, and of a red rose colour, having a crown of red gilly flowers upon his head. His face looketh upwards to heaven and is of a red colour, and is compassed round about with a bright splendour as the beams of the sun. Before he departeth he speaketh unto the exorcist saying, I am your friend and brother. And illuminateth the air round about with his splendour, and leaveth a pleasant smell which will last a long time upon their heads.

OF THE THIRD CHORA OR ALTITUDE

In this chora you must do in all things as you were before directed in the other two. The angels in this Altitude are named, viz: ELIPHANIASAI,   GELOMIROS,   GEDOBONAI, TARANAVA & ELOMINA.

They appear in the form of little children or little women dressed in green and silver colours very delightful to behold, and a crown of baye leaf with white and colours upon their heads. And they seem to look a little downwards with their faces. And they speak as the others do to the exorcist, and leave a mighty sweet perfume behind them.

OF THE FOURTH CHORA OR ALTITUDE

In this Chora you must do as before in the others, and the Angels in this Chora are called BARCAHIEL, GEDIEL, GEDIEL, DELIEL and CAPITIEL. They appear in the form of little men or boys, with clothes of a black colour mixed with a dark green; and in their hands they hold a bird which is naked; and their heads compassed round about with a bright shining of divers colours. They leave a sweet smell behind them, but differ from the others something.

THE TIMES FOR INVOKING THE ANGELS

Note there is twelve Princes, beside those in the four Altitudes: and they distribute their offices amongst themselves, every one ruling thirty days every year. Now it will be in vain to call any of the Angels unless it be those that govern then, for every Chora or altitude hath its limited time, according to the twelve signs of the Zodiack; and in that Sign the Sun is in, that or those Angels that belong to that Sign hath the government [and should be invoked]. As, for example: suppose that I would call the 2 first of the 5 that belong to the first Chora. Then choose the first Sunday in March, after the Sun hath entered Aries: and then I make an experiment. And so do the like, if you will, the next Sunday after again. And if you will call the two second that belong to the first Chora, that Sunday after the Sun enters Taurus in April. But if you will call the last of the 5, then you must take those Sundays that are in May after the Sun has entered Gemini, to make your experiment in. Do the like in the other Altitudes, for they have all one way of working. But the Altitudes have names formed severally in the substance of the heavens, even a Character. For when the Angels hear the names of God that is attributed to them, they hear it by virtue of that Character. Therefore it is in vain to call any angel or spirit unless he knows what name to call him by. Therefore observe the form of this conjuration or invocation following:

THE INVOCATION

"O thou great, blessed and glorious Angel of God (N), who rulest and is the chief governing Angel in the (number) Chora or Altitude. I am the servant of the Highest, the same your God ADONAIJ, HELOMI, AND PINE,1 whom you do obey, and is your distributor and disposer of all things both in heaven earth and hell, do invocate, conjure and entreat you (N) that thou forthwith appear in the virtue and power of the same God, ADONAIJ, HELOMI AND PINE; and I do command thee by him whom ye do obey, and is set over you as King in the divine power of God, that you forthwith descend from thy orders or place of abode to come unto me, and show thyself visibly here before me in this crystal stone, in thy own proper shape and glory, speaking with a voice intelligible to my understanding.

"O thou mighty and powerful Angel (N), who art by the power of God ordained to govern all animals, vegetables and minerals, and to cause them and all creatures of God to spring increase and bring forth according to their kinds and natures: I, the servant of the Most High God whom you obey, do entreat and humbly beseech thee to come from your celestial mansion, and shew unto me all things I shall desire of you, so far as in office you may or can or is capable to perform, if God permit to the same.

"O thou servant of mercy (N), I do humbly entreat and beseech thee by these holy and blessed names of your God ADONAIJ, HELLOMI, PINE; And I do also constrain you in and by this powerful name ANABONA, that you forthwith appear visibly and plainly in your own proper shape and glory in and through this crystal stone, that I may visibly see you, and audibly hear you speak unto me, and that I may have thy blessed and glorious angelic assistance, familiar friendship and constant society, community and instruction, both now and at all times, to inform and rightly instruct me in my ignorance and depraved intellect, judgement and understanding, and to assist me both herein and in all other truths also, through the Almighty ADONAIJ, King of Kings, the giver of all good gifts that his bountiful and fatherly mercy be graciously pleased to bestow upon me. Therefore, O thou blessed Angel (N), be friendly unto me, so far as God shall give you power and presence, to appear, that I may sing with his holy Angels.

"O Mappa Laman, Hallelujah. Amen. When he appears, give him or them kind entertainment; and then ask what is just and lawful, and that which is proper and suitable to his office. And you shall obtain it.

SO ENDETH THE 4TH BOOK CALLED THE ALMADEL OF SOLOMON THE KING

THE ARS NOVA
THE FIRST PAGE

Eheie. Kether. Almighty God, whose dwelling is in the highest Heavens: Haioth. The great King of Heaven, and of all the powers therein: Methratton. And of all the holy hosts of Angels and Archangels: Reschith. Hear the prayers of Thy servant who putteth his trust in Thee: Hagalgalim. Let thy Holy Angels be commanded to assist me at this time and at all times. — (Sphere of the Primum Mobile)

Iehovah. God Almighty, God Omnipotent, hear my prayer: Hadonat. Command Thy Holy Angels above the fixed stars: Ophanim. To be assisting and aiding Thy servant: Iophiel. That I may command all spirits of air, water, fire, earth, and hell: Masloth. So that it may tend unto Thy glory and unto the good of man. — S. Z. (Sphere of the Zodiac)

Iehovah. God Almighty, God Omnipotent, hear my prayer: Elohim. God with us, God be always present with us: Binah. Strengthen us and support us, both now and for ever: Aralim. In these our undertakings, which we perform but as instruments in Thy hands: Zabbathai In the hands of Thee, the great God of Sabaoth. — S. H.

Hesel3 Thou great God, governor and creator of the planets, and of the Host of Heaven: Hasmalim Command them by Thine almighty power: Zelez To be now present and assisting to us Thy poor servants, both now and for ever. — K. S.

Elohim Geber Most Almighty and eternal and ever living Lord God: Seraphim Command Thy Seraphim: Camael, Madim To attend on us now at this time, to assist us, and to defend us from all perils and dangers. — S. _

Eloha O Almighty God! be present with us both now and for ever: Tetragrammaton And let thine Almighty power and presence ever guard and protect us now and for ever: Raphael Let thy holy angel Raphael wait upon us at this present and for ever: Schemes To assist us in these our undertakings. — S.

Iehovah. God Almighty, God Omnipotent, hear my prayer: Sabaoth. Thou great God of Sabaoth: Netzah All-seeing God: Elohim. God be present with us, and let thy presence be now and always present with us: Haniel. Let thy holy angel Haniel come and minister unto us at this present. — S. _

Elohim. O God! be present with us, and let thy presence be now and alway present with us: Sabaoth. O thou great God of Sabaoth, be present with us at this time and for ever: Hodben Let Thine Almighty power defend us and protect us, both now and for ever: Michael. Let Michael, who is, under Thee, general of thy heavenly host: Cochab. Come and expel all evil and danger from us both now and for ever. — S.

Sadai. Thou great God of all wisdom and knowledge: Jesah Instruct Thy poor and most humble servant: Cherubim. Thy holy Cherubim: Gabriel. By Thy Holy Angel Gabriel, who is the Author and Messenger of good tidings: Levanah. Direct and support us at this present and for ever. — S.

THE EXPLANATION OF THE TWO TRIANGLES IN THE PARCHMENT

Alpha & Omega Thou, O great God, Who art the beginning and the end:

Tetragrammaton Thou God of Almighty power, be ever present with us to guard and protect us, and let Thy Holy Spirit and presence be now and always with us:

Tetragrammaton Thou God of Almighty power, be ever present with us to guard and protect us, and let Thy Holy Spirit and presence be now and always with us:

Soluzen. I command thee, thou Spirit, of whatsoever region thou art, to come unto this circle:

Halliza And appear in human shape: Bellator And speak unto us audibly in our mother-tongue:

Bellonoy (or Bellony) And show, and discover unto us all treasure that thou knowest of, or that is in thy keeping, and deliver it unto us quietly:

Hally Fra And answer all such questions as we may demand without any defect now at this time.

AN EXPLANATION OF SOLOMON'S TRIANGLE

Anephezeton. Thou great God of all the Heavenly Host:

Tetragrammaton. Thou God of Almighty power, be ever present with us to guard and protect us, and let Thy Holy Spirit and presence be now and always with us:

Primeumaton. Thou Who art the First and Last, let all spirits be subject unto us, and let the Spirit be bound in this triangle, that disturbs this place:

Michael. By Thy Holy Angel Michael, until I shall discharge him.

THE ARS NOVA
THE SECOND PAGE

ש Jodgea הדו׳ל׳ Rosen Emolack

לכב Rosen Subbartha אלבל Rosen Eloham גׄלׄכׄלׄד

Skimoy Abomoth לבל Rosen Elemoth

אל ל Zadon דׄלׄללׄל Behoma Reson

אׄול Gamaliall דׄלׄל Mackhamasack

לבׄלׄ Baseh Zadon ל Hinmore

עלד Molock Ehaddon

אׄל אׄל הׄל Molack Johiron & Michael

Jodgea, I humbly implore thee Rosen Emolack thou everlasting
god Roson Subbartha thou omnipotent & everlasting Creator
Roson Eloham thou god with us Skimoy Abomoth to bind & keep
fast Rosen Elemoth Mackhamasmack by thy divine power those
evil & airy spirits Baseh Zadon of the spirit of flyes & spirit of the
air Hinnon & spirit of Hinnon Molock Ehaddon with all the spirits
of hidden treasure & the disturbers of mankind Molack with the
spirits of Molack Johinnon in chains in thy brazen urn Michael
with thy Arch Angel Michael.....

THE MIGHTY ORATION

By the most great & almighty power of Alpha & Omega, Jehovah &
Emmanuel, and by him that divided the Red Sea & by that great
power that turned all the waters & rivers of Egypt into blood &
turned all the dust into flies & chains & by that great power that
brought frogs all over the land of Egypt & entered into the King's
Palace & chambers & by that great power that terrible thunder &
lightning & hail stones mixt with fire, & sent locusts which did
destroy all growing things in the whole land of Egypt, & by that
great power that destroyed all the first born of the land of Egypt

both of man & beast, & by that great power that divided the hard rock & rivers of water issued out of the sand of the wilderness, and by that great power that led the children of Israel into the land of Canaan & by that great power that destroyed Sonachoribs great host & by that great & almighty power of him that walked on the sea as on dry land, & by that almighty power that raised the dead Lazarus out of his grave, & by that almighty power of the blessed & holy & glorious trinity that did cast the Devil & all disobedient Angels out of heaven into hell that thou thief return immediately & restore the goods again which thou hast stolen away, therefore in & by the names of the Almighty God before rehearsed I charge thee, thou thief to restore the goods again immediately or else the wrath of God may fall upon thee & force thee to come immediately. Amen.

SO ENDETH THE 5TH BOOK CALLED THE NOVA OF SOLOMON THE KING

www.ingramcontent.com/pod-product-compliance
Lightning Source LLC
Chambersburg PA
CBHW051944090426
42741CB00008B/1264